Journey to the
Forbidden China

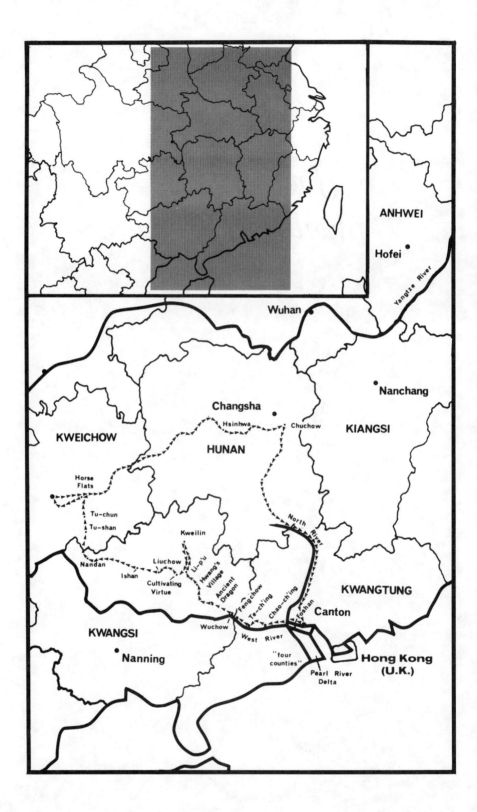

Journey to the Forbidden China

Steven W. Mosher

THE FREE PRESS
A Division of Macmillan, Inc.
NEW YORK

Collier Macmillan Publishers
LONDON

The Free Press
A Division of Macmillan, Inc.
866 Third Avenue, New York, N. Y. 10022

Collier Macmillan Canada, Inc.

Printed in the United States of America

printing number
1   2   3   4   5   6   7   8   9   10

Library of Congress Cataloging in Publication Data

Mosher, Steven W.
  Journey to the forbidden China.

  1. China—Description and travel—1976-
2. China—Social life and customs—1976-
3. Mosher, Steven W.   I. Title.
DS712.M675   1985   951.05′8   85-2610
ISBN 0-02-921710-5

For my driver, Ming,
who knew the way

Just as the weary traveler despairs of finding a road, lo, a village appears and the shade of willows and riotous flowers beckon.

—Sung dynasty poem

Where a great proportion of the people are suffered to languish in helpless misery, that country must be ill-policed and wretchedly governed: a decent provision for the poor is the true test of civilization.

—James Boswell, *The Life of Samuel Johnson*

Contents

Prologue

Nᴏᴛ long before leaving for China in March 1979, I went to the
health center at Stanford University, where I was a doctoral candidate
in anthropology, to see what inoculations my journey required. I would
be staying in a village in the South China countryside, I explained to the
nurse on duty, and I didn't want to come down with any virulent tropical diseases. "I'll give you all recommended inoculations," she
responded with brisk efficiency, reaching for the thick World Health
Organization publication on her desk. She quickly found the entry for
the People's Republic of China, but then pursed her lips in bewilder-
ment. "Well I'll be," she said finally. "They don't seem to have any information on China." She beckoned me over and pointed to the rele-
vant table. It was blank. Etched on my mind is the accompanying out-
line map of China, on which should have appeared information on the
spatial distribution of the major infectious diseases like smallpox, yellow
fever, cholera, typhoid, and malaria. Instead, in the middle of the map,
beckoning to me like some landlocked Bermuda triangle, was a giant
question mark.

I found this "nonmap" amusing at the time (though considerably
less so after the nurse dourly resolved to give me shots for practically
everything as a precautionary measure), but I gradually came to see it as

1

the symbol par excellence of the dismal state of our knowledge about rural China. Gradually emerging from its cultural isolation after the Opium Wars of the last century, China was once again plunged into seclusion when the xenophobic Mao Tse-tung came to power and imposed a quarantine on unsupervised contact with the West. Only Party-controlled outlets like the *Peking Review* or the colorful *China Reconstructs* were given license to communicate with the West, and their euphoric reports about the socialist miracles occurring in the countryside under collectivization, their pictures of peasants of tubular physique laboring in the fields with an air of ecstasy, strained credulity to its limits. The outside world was left to wonder, increasingly as time went on, what life was really like for the hundreds of millions of peasants under their new masters. The vastness of agrarian China had, like the map in the inoculation handbook, been reduced to the single dimension of a question mark.

Even after China embarked on its abortive Great Leap Westward in the late seventies and early eighties, the countryside continued to be sealed off from the prying eyes of foreigners. Boeing 747s now flew directly from New York to Peking, but foreign residents of the Chinese capital were still cloistered in guarded compounds. The number of tourists reached 125,000 in 1978, more than in all the previous years since 1949, but they all danced along the same string of approved cities and carefully scrubbed historical sites.[1] Under the aegis of the Sino-American Cultural Exchange Agreement that was signed following the normalization of diplomatic relations, I was permitted to live in the countryside for nearly a year in 1979–1980. Far more typical, however, was the experience of Peking-based correspondents like Fox Butterfield, whose repeated requests to visit villages for more than the brief inspection tours of model communes permitted by the authorities were rebuffed. The government even refused his application for permission to visit me in the village where I was doing research, though I had made it clear that I welcomed visitors and could have provided transportation and lodging. "It was almost as if there was something secret about the peasants that the government wanted to hide," Butterfield concluded.[2]

[1] 1978 was the first year of regular tourism. By 1981 the number of visitors had risen to 218,000.

[2] Fox Butterfield, *China: Alive in a Bitter Sea* (New York: Times Books, 1982), p. 238.

This compulsive cloaking of conditions in the countryside was all the more surprising in view of the close, almost symbiotic relationship that the Communists had claimed to have with the peasantry. Certainly there can be no doubt that the Communist Party owed a blood debt to the countryside. Early attempts to foment urban unrest, most notably Mao's 1927 Autumn Harvest Uprising, had been bloody debacles. It was only after the center of Party agitation had shifted to the rural masses that the movement began to show signs of success. Rural backwaters like Ching-kang-shan, a mountainous region on the borders of Hunan and Kiangsi provinces, the Right River Soviet in northwest Kwangsi province, and Yenan, in the parched, impoverished Chinese northwest, were the first areas to come under Communist control. The cities were the last. During the decades-long civil war that separated these momentous events, it was the poor farmers of areas like Yenan who provided shelter, rice, and recruits for the Red armies. It was on the strong backs of China's peasants that the Communists rode to power.

For their part, Mao Tse-tung and the other Communist leaders consciously and carefully cultivated an image of oneness with the peasantry. They recognized the "peasant problem" as their own, boldly proclaiming that they were going to liberate the peasantry for all time from "feudal exploitation." In the areas the Communists controlled, land rents were reduced, the poorer peasants were organized, and landowners, when they were not summarily executed, were stripped of all property they could not farm themselves. After the establishment of the People's Republic, Mao himself pledged that the Party would take agriculture as the "foundation" of China's economic development. The redistribution of farmland was completed in the 1952 Land Reform, and the formation of mutual-aid teams and collectives followed. By the time that rural communes were established in 1958, the reconstruction of the countryside seemed well underway. More recently, Vice Premier Teng Hsiao-p'ing, who rose to power following Mao's death, has identified agriculture as one of the four cornerstones of China's modernization, and he has talked of per capita incomes reaching US$800 by the year 2000. The Communist leaders had kept their promise to the peasantry—or had they?

I had not been in China long before I began to suspect that there was something vastly amiss in the countryside. The village in the Pearl

River Delta where I went to live had been favored by nature. Tropical fruits such as lichees, pineapples, and bananas flourished in a climate that permitted farming year-round; river channels criss-crossed the low-lying land, bringing an unfailing supply of water for irrigation; black bottom mud from canals and ponds provided an inexhaustible source of natural fertilizer; the fecund alluvial soil faithfully yielded up bounteous harvests season after season, year after year. In all of China, only communes that lay near sizable southern cities, benefiting from abundant supplies of night soil and specializing in labor-intensive truck farming, could rival this agricultural cornucopia in production, and none could surpass it. It was the native wealth of the Delta, known throughout Kwangtung in preliberation times as "little gold mountain," that accounted for the central government's willingness to let me observe life there in the first place. Yet I found the lives of my peasant neighbors in this land of plenty to be achingly impoverished. They wore clothes of rationed cloth, lived in simple brick homes without heat or running water, and, most surprising of all, sat down to meals of usually nothing more than steamed rice and salted vegetables. It was a land where frugality was not virtue but necessity, where electric lights could not be used during daylight hours, where worn-out sweaters were not discarded but unraveled and the yarn reused, where burnt-out teakettles were not thrown away but had new bottoms painstakingly hammered and soldered onto their boilers by itinerant tinsmiths.[3]

It did not take me long to see that what prevented the local peasants from realizing their natural prosperity was nothing other than the Communist state itself. Direct state levies on local earnings, it was true, were low, amounting to only 7 percent or so of a collective's annual income. The real squeeze was more subtle. For nearly two hundred years, ever since the Ch'ien-lung Emperor in 1757 made Canton the sole port for foreign trade, the villagers of the Delta had raised freshwater fish and silkworms, earning a comfortable living from the sale of their fish and silk in the markets of Canton and later Hong Kong. After the revolution, however, the state gradually moved to take control of the production and marketing of these important commercial crops. Mandatory

[3] I have described Chinese peasant life in *Broken Earth: The Rural Chinese* (New York: The Free Press, 1983).

quotas for production were set, with purchase prices well below fair market value. The results of this systematic exploitation—and here I choose my words as carefully as I can—are enormous turnaround profits for the state and a depressed standard of living for the peasantry. Delta villagers are fully aware that their incomes are well below what they should be if their produce sold freely on the open market as it once did. Where their grandfathers dressed in silk and feasted on fish, the villagers of today are clad in cotton broadcloth and have become vegetarians by default. When asked how their lives could be improved, my village friends responded like good Libertarians by calling for less government intervention. "Let us grow what we want and sell what we grow," one woman said bluntly, spreading her hands wide as if calling for a totalitarian state to relax its grip were the most natural thing in the world.

My village, notwithstanding its needless poverty, was still quite wealthy by mainland Chinese standards. This was driven home to me early in my stay when I was visited by a high-ranking cadre in the Ministry of Education. It took only a brief walk around the village to have this normally inscrutable official shaking his head in amazement over "how rich the peasants here are." And he was in a position to know, for like many Peking officials he had spent several years during the Cultural Revolution laboring with hoe and carrying pole in the North China countryside.

However pathetic the local per capita income of $110 seemed to me initially, the discovery that this sum was nearly double what the average Chinese peasant received forced me to view it in a different light. The PRC's own State Statistical Bureau reported that per capita peasant income from work in the collective fields was just $57 in 1980, a figure that could only err on the side of optimism. Other statistics released by Peking confirmed the Pearl River Delta's prosperity. Only a quarter of China's five million production teams—the lowest level of collective agricultural organization, under the brigades and communes—had per capita incomes over $67 that same year, a figure easily exceeded by even the poorest of Delta teams. And most teams in China did much worse. Half fell between $67 and $33 per head, while those in the bottom quartile provided less than $33 to their team members, primarily in the form of distributions of grain and other collectively cultivated crops. For the hundreds of millions of peasants living at or near the $27 a year (equivalent to 320 pounds of grain or rice) that Peking calculates as necessary to stave off starvation, I saw that the spartan but stable Delta diet of rice and vegetables must seem appetizing indeed. But in general I was too taken aback by the straitened circumstances of the supposedly wealthy villagers I worked among to imagine the human reality hinted at by the dismal statistics concerning other peasants.

Still, I occasionally caught hard glimpses of peasant life outside the Delta. My village was located along the Hsi Chiang or West River, which marks the western boundary of the delta. Across its mile-wide waters lay hill country. If the Pearl River Delta had been favored by nature, then the hill country on the opposite bank—rugged of contour, poor of soil, and difficult of irrigation—had been shortchanged by it. Like the larger district of which it was a part, called in Cantonese the "four counties," the opposite bank early came to specialize in the export of the only local resource that was both abundant and under utilized: able-bodied men. Most American Chinese and many Southeast Asian Chinese are the descendants of coolie laborers who emigrated from this and other parts of the four counties from the mid-1800s onward. The movement overseas ended with the establishment of the PRC, and in 1958 even Chinese cities and towns were barred to would-be peasant immigrants. The effect was to bind the people of the four counties—and peasants throughout China—to their native villages, perpetuating preexisting inequalities between adjacent communities and districts. Even after the coming of the communes, the West River remained a watershed of wealth, with "four counties" peasants earning only half as much as their cross-river countrymen.

It was several decades before outside opportunity beckoned again, and when it did, it came from the nearby Delta. Many brigades and communes there, taking advantage of the fine alluvial soil, their relative plentitude of capital, and the more relaxed economic policies of Teng Hsiao-p'ing, had built large, labor-intensive brickworks in the late 1970s. Rather unexpectedly in the densely populated Delta, labor had proved to be a problem. Although local youths were willing to run the mechanical brick press, fire the kiln, or even stack bricks for drying and firing, for the most part they refused to dig and haul to the press the carts of clayey soil needed, contemptuously dismissing this task as fit only for "cow and horse." Instead of inducing the youths to work by raising wages or improving working conditions, commune factory managers behaved like unenlightened capitalists: They brought in cheap labor from across the river. These "black laborers," so called because they lacked local population registration and could live and work in the Delta only illegally, were almost pathetically grateful for the opportunity to labor as beasts of burden. The one yuan (about fifty cents) a day that local youth had scorned was, after all, three times what such labor was worth on the opposite bank and moreover was paid in hard cash instead of grain. It would hardly have occurred to these cheerful, unassuming, and hard-working young men to reflect on the historical irony of their situation, that more than a century after their ancestors had shipped out as coolies to distant America they had been moved by the same unremitting poverty to become coolies next door to home.

On another occasion I listened to a young schoolteacher's litany of rural life in even more remote regions. As punishment for her activism in the Canton Red Guards during the Cultural Revolution, she had been banished to a distant mountain commune in northwestern Kwangtung in 1970. She was still assigned there at the time I spoke with her ten years later, although now she was no longer restricted to the commune but was allowed to visit Delta relatives on her infrequent vacations. Despite her long exile, she was not bitter, but after the best Chinese fashion had come to terms with her lot.

"The area I was sent to had a long revolutionary history," she told me in her appealingly direct manner. "One of the first soviets in all of Kwangtung was set up there forty years ago. But they are still as poor as they have always been."

"In what way?"

"There are no roads, just paths that go back into the mountains. There is no electricity or kerosene, so that the peasants go to bed as soon as it gets dark. There are no wells. Drinking water has to be brought in from a stream a mile away."

"What do the peasants eat?"

"Corn and sweet potatoes. Cooking oil, salt, and vinegar are in short supply. Rice and pork are eaten only five or six times a year on festival days."

This witness went on to tell of earthen-floored huts, of solitary garments that must be patched and repatched, of disease and early death. It was a sobering tale of misery and destitution. But still I wanted to be sure.

"Surely some things must have changed for the better. Take education. You had been sent there to teach."

She reflected on this for a moment and shook her head. "No, I was sent there as punishment."

"But you do teach."

"Yes, I teach in a lower primary school. Grades one through four. But it does no good. Few of my pupils go on to upper primary school. There is no hope. It is hard for you to understand how miserable the people are because you have not lived there."

"But I have seen 'four counties' villages."

She smiled. "That's a wealthy area compared to where I live. They eat rice. They have roads. They have soy sauce. They have soap. No, I mean the really back-of-the-mountain villages. You haven't seen them and so you can't know."

So it became clear to me that I had landed in an anomalous pocket of prosperity. Without venturing out into the surrounding wilderness of poverty, I knew that I could not answer what I saw as the two most critical questions surrounding the Communist Chinese revolution: During the three decades it has been in power, what has the Chinese Communist Party done for the peasantry to which it owes—and has promised—so much? And during the decades to come, will the Chinese peasantry be able to achieve the agricultural modernization and rising incomes pledged by Teng's Four Modernizations program?

For the sake of the Chinese, a people for whom I had come to feel as great an affection as I felt for my own, I would like to have been able to give positive, upbeat answers to these questions. But after a year of living in the Pearl River Delta, my evaluation of the revolution's past achievements vis-à-vis the peasantry was decidedly mixed, my prognosis of its prospects pessimistic. From the Chinese themselves I had come to see the state's relationship with the villages as essentially predatory. Heavy indirect taxes and a ban on almost all economic activity except producing for the state had so shackled peasant enterprise and initiative that it had only been in the year or two prior to my arrival, when Teng had loosened these restrictions, that the peasants had at long last begun to gradually improve their lot. Even the social programs in rural education and health care, so often touted as evidence of benefits that the Communists have brought to the countryside, turned out on closer inspection to be bootstrap operations paid for out of community coffers and staffed by local personnel. All of this suggested to me that, like the Russian kulaks, the prosperous Delta peasantry had not been saved by the revolution so much as sacrificed to it.

But I could not rule out the possibility that more inhospitable parts of the countryside had seen marked improvement, either because once upon a time peasant conditions had been so bad that even modest achievements shone by comparison, or because the Communist regime had made more of an effort to ameliorate living conditions in the worst regions in the name of socialist equality. If more advanced regions like the Delta had been held back, then it was at least conceivable that more backward areas had made rapid progress. The exiled teacher was right. I had to see for myself.

So it was that as the end of my stay in the village approached, I began to think of making an extensive motor trip into the heartland of South China. As I envisioned the journey, it would take me from Kwangtung province on the South China Sea to Szechwan province in the remove interior. I would follow the West River out of the Delta westward, up the winding gorges and wide hollows of the river's middle reaches to the city of Wuchow in Kwangsi province. From there I would strike out northwestward for the city of Chungking in Szechwan, on a route that would take me up through the hill-and-valley landscape of Kwangsi and across the high and barren plateau of Yunkwei before my descent into the remote basin that was Szechwan. Afterwards I would go down the Yangtze River by boat to the cities of Shanghai and Nanking, and then north by rail to Peking, exiting China by air at journey's end. There would be time to relax during these latter stages of my journey, but the first leg of the trip, the gradual, tortuous ascent from Kwangtung to Kweichow, would be anything but restful.

Kwangtung, the best-known of China's provinces and my starting point, is for the most part a country of river deltas and rolling hills under 1,000 feet. Inland elevations grow. Kwangsi is a province of narrow valleys and steep-sided mountains that climb to over 3,000 feet in the west where the province abuts the Yunkwei Plateau. It is here, on a rugged tableland that ranges from 3,000 to 6,000 feet in elevation, that Kweichow province is located.

Kweichow has long been the most isolated and backward of China's provinces. Snow-covered peaks, tropical jungles, verticle-walled canyons, and warlike tribes combined to forestall immigration for centuries. Long after the lush, lowland valleys of the four surrounding provinces of Szechwan, Hunan, Kwangsi, and Yunnan had been settled by Han Chinese, Kweichow was home to only a relatively small number of soldiers, officials, and traders. Unlike other remote parts of China, Kweichow did not even serve as a way station. Kansu in the north held the attractions of the Silk Road, over which camel caravans carried Chinese silks across Central Asia to Rome; Szechwan stood astride the way to exotic Tibet; even remote Yunnan led on to Burma. Kweichow led nowhere, and was bypassed. So inaccessible did the provincial capital of Kweiyang remain, even in the 1920s, that when the first automobiles were brought into the province it was necessary to completely dismantle the vehicles and have the parts carried in by coolies over ancient trails.

Even less was known about changes in more recent years. *Nagel's Guide to China* dismissed the province in only four pages (three of which were devoted to Kweiyang), far less than it gave to any other. Kweichow was a high mountain fastness that few foreigners had ever wanted to visit. I did, for the trip from Kwangtung to Kweichow would constitute a perfect transect from wealth to poverty—unless the Communist Party had invented a new calculus of rural well-being. It would be a journey into a China long hidden from Western eyes.

It was one thing to imagine making such a journey; it was quite another to gain permission for it from a secretive and security-conscious totalitarian state. I did not want to travel by rail or air—the standard forms of transportation for foreigners in China—because that would close off the countryside to me. Buses were also out because in China there is no national bus network equivalent to Greyhound or Continental. Each city is the hub of a bus system that serves its own transportation needs, and its buses rarely go farther than the next city and almost never to the next province. To understand the changes that had taken place in rural life, I would have to travel by motor vehicle. I told my driver, Ming, to prepare my van for a long journey, and went to seek official permission.

I began by discussing my trip with my official liaison at the Kwangtung Provincial Department of Foreign Affairs, Wen Ming-lu. Comrade Wen had no questions about my wish to visit Kweilin, Chungking, and other cities, and a thirty-day visa for the period of my trip was stamped in my passport. But my request to travel by van was not to be so easily approved.

"The foreign affairs department is not sure if it will be convenient for you to travel by van," Wen began smoothly. "It's already so hot in China by June that you may find such a long motor trip unpleasant. Besides, the food in the countryside is unsanitary."

I had been half expecting Wen to turn my request down outright, and was relieved to find that he was worried primarily about my comfort and health, always concerns of the Chinese when dealing with foreigners. "On the road we'll have a breeze so it won't be too hot," I reassured him. "We'll also be careful about where and what we eat. I've taken many long trips by car before."

"Of course you have," Wen interjected, "but China is not America. Some of our roads in the interior are very bad. It might be very uncomfortable for you."

"I've been using the van for seven months now," I responded, beginning to wonder where all of Wen's objections were leading. "It rides well. I have been all over the Delta with it, as you know."

"Yes, you have, certainly, certainly," Wen agreed hurriedly. "But the foreign affairs department is worried about your taking such a long trip by van." Here Wen paused and nervously pinched his chin between thumb and forefinger before adding in a low, hesitant voice, "It may not be safe."

It may not be safe? His words stunned me. I had been in the People's Republic long enough to have heard tales of roving guerrilla gangs, but this was the first time an official had admitted to me that it might not be safe to venture out alone too far away from the cities. Or was this just an indirect refusal of my request? I decided to try one last time.

"Groups of Hong Kong Chinese often rent vans for the trip to Kweilin," I parried. "At least that route must be safe."

A flicker of misgiving passed quickly across Wen's usually impassive face, and he shifted uncomfortably in his chair. What was the man trying to communicate? When he finally spoke, he was abrupt. ''The foreign affairs department does not have the authority to give you permission to travel by van. Only public security can do that. You can make your request to them when you apply for your travel permit.''

I went to the public security office early the next day. Without much hope that the request would be granted, I stated on the travel application form that I wanted to travel by motor vehicle for the first part of my trip, and then use train, ship, and plane for the rest. To my surprise, the public security cadre who reviewed the form did not raise his eyebrows at my request to travel by van, asking only in his dry, paper-shuffling voice how far I intended to travel by that mode of transportation. Nor did he blink when I said ''Szechwan,'' imperturbably jotting down on the form the name of that distant province. Form completed, he disappeared upstairs without a word. My spirits had been strangely bouyed by his very neutrality.

When he finally returned he was carrying a travel permit, a little green folded card that he handed to me without comment. I flipped it open to ''means of transportation,'' and the words ''motor vehicle'' leaped out at me. Awash in a sudden sense of spaciousness, mystery, and adventure, I barely remembered to thank the cadre. I was about to become the first foreigner in thirty years to journey unescorted into the rural heartland of China and I was going to find out the truth about the revolution and the peasants.

CHAPTER ONE

Underway

CURIOUS passersby stopped and stared as, travel permit in hand and a smile on my face, I walked out of the Canton Municipal Department of Public Security. How puzzled they must be, I realized, to see someone emerging from Public Security, the police and Chinese KGB rolled into one, in such good spirits. Most Chinese, in their dealings with the police, followed the ancient advice given by Confucius concerning ghosts. "Be respectful but keep your distance," the Sage had admonished. And here I was smiling. But my driver, Ming, understood. As I bounded into the waiting van, he greeted me with a smile of his own, an easy, slightly sardonic expression that fit him well. Almost before I had finished saying "To the West River," he had slid the van into gear and pulled out into the traffic of Liberation Road. We were underway.

I would soon be quit of Canton. Certainly the City of the Rams had its charms, not the least of which is this legend that the city was founded by five men riding on as many rams, a fancy that is given form by a carving of the intertwined quintuplet that graces the central park. But I had visited the city repeatedly during the past year and had early exhausted its offerings, few for a city of two million: the city zoo, where dull-eyed animals stood in cages too small for comfort; the Peasant Institute, where Mao had taught in the twenties, now a museum; the Park of Surpassing Refinement; the North Garden Restaurant. The zoo and restaurant I had visited again just a few days earlier in the company of rural friends. The main attraction for me had been seeing my companions' mouths form into small "o"'s of astonishment at the elephant, a creature of myth become flesh and blood, and watching them confront a banquet where no rice was served, their chopsticks hovering uncertainly in the air despite my entreaties to eat because they had been taught that it is immodest to take less than three mouthfuls of rice for every one of meat or vegetables, for rice is cheap and these other foods dear. In their simplicity they had offered me poignant glimpses of the pastoral, giving further point to my planned journey.

Now embarked, we wouldn't stop until we were far from the City of the Rams, validating our resolve to travel by quickly putting some distance between us and our starting point. However meandering an odyssey later becomes, it always starts with a sense of hurried purpose.

No one would have guessed that the Mazda passenger van we were riding in had been imported spanking new from Hong Kong only six months before. It had taken only a few days in the village for me to realize that if I didn't want to lapse into the anchorite existence of my peasant neighbors, I had to have better transportation. It took an hour to hike to the nearest village, nearly that to cycle to the commune headquarters, and the bus trip into Canton took the better part of a day. But with the van came mishaps. A few weeks after its arrival, Ming had rammed a foot-thick Great Leap Forward tree rather than hit an errant cyclist and had flattened the left front fender down to the frame. Three months later an apprentice driver—not Ming—had fishtailed in the loose sand surface of a dike road and flipped the van stunt-like into the sugarcane patch below, pleating the roof into accordian folds. Along narrow country roads, in the crush of market towns, and on board tiny river ferries, its once-bright finish had become a cobblework of nicks and scratches. After each mishap, large or small, Ming had made such repairs to the crumpled sheet metal as could be effected with hammer and crowbar, and had even painted over the scarred paint with an off-color enamel. The van nevertheless bore the look of an aging prizefighter who has gone a few rounds too many.

Though the van had been disfigured by its collisions, it had not been disabled, and because of Ming's constant and careful maintenance I was confident that it remained basically sound. Where we were going it would have to be. A serious breakdown would strand us along some cart path in the remote interior of China, far from hope of repair. Even if we were somehow able to get the car to a garage in some county town, the mechanics there would probably throw up their hands at the foreign vehicle, not that they would have any spare parts for a 1980 Mazda passenger van in any event. We carried our repair shop with us, for we had no alternative. A large crate in the back of the van contained two inner tubes, a hand pump, plugs, a rotor, a coil, and a distributor cap, as well as a number of more exotic parts that Ming had managed to scavenge or trade for. Ming's tool kit and two spare tires sat to one side.

Another box contained food that I had brought in from Hong Kong for the trip: canned meats, boxes of biscuits, and cartons of sterilized milk, along with two thermos bottles of potable water. We also carried bedrolls—cotton quilts rolled up inside of large rice mats—though Ming smilingly cautioned that, because of the danger involved, we would spend the night in the van only as a last resort. But our most precious cargo, strapped securely down in the very back of the van, was three fifty-liter cans of gasoline. Like many goods in China's centrally controlled economy, gas was distributed under a strict quota system, not sold freely at gas stations. There was only one station in all of Canton, the one serving the small foreign community, and even there it took not just cash but ration coupons to make a purchase. We knew that we would not find it easy to purchase gas along the way, so we carried our own. It was enough, Ming calculated, to take us to Chungking.

As I surveyed Ming's careful preparations, I reflected again upon my good fortune in having him as my driver on this trip. Even though he was only, like myself, in his early thirties, Ming had some fifteen years of experience behind the wheel, including eight years as a truck driver for the People's Liberation Army, and had hauled freight all over central and South China. During the six months he had been driving for me in the Delta, I had found him to be a skillful driver—he could scarcely be faulted for his mishap with the tree—and an experienced mechanic Chinese-style, as able to make a resourceful horse trade for a needed spare part as to make the van run without it. Like his fellow drivers, Ming was as much a rugged individualist as a crowded, collectivist country like China could produce. In a society where a travel permit is necessary to leave one's commune or city limits, a driver is free to travel the length and breadth of China on the strength of his driver's license alone; where others keep common hours and labor under cadre supervision, a driver on assignment can choose his own route and stopovers. He can even do a little black market trading on the side, profiting in the odd, eternal scarcities that crop up in a command economy. Drivers were thus a special breed, independent, free-thinking, and self-reliant. Ming possessed these driver's traits in spades, plus an alert intelligence that had easily escaped the bounds of his sixth-grade rural education. But to me his most attractive characteristic was a curiously sardonic sense of humor, which found expression even in silence by a permanent half-smile, as if he were ever amused by some one or other little absurdity of life. It was the look of a man who has seen—and seen through—everything. Every pilgrim needs a guide, and given the nature of my quest, I could not have asked for a better traveling companion.

Shortly after we crossed over the Pearl River and turned west onto the road to Foshan, the city ended. The transition was abrupt, as it always is in China, where urbs do not sprawl endlessly over the landscape as they do in the West. One second we were passing grey blocks of urban housing. The next we had entered the suburban garden belt that encircled the city of Canton and provided its two million residents with fresh vegetables. The land to either side of the arrow-straight road was a patchwork quilt of plots of leeks, turnips, eggplants, cucumbers, and spinach, as well as more exotic items such as bak choi (Chinese cabbage) and lotus root. Government-owned tractors pulling trailers piled high with produce bound for the state-run vegetable markets of Canton went noisily chugging by, leaving puffs of grey smoke hanging in the air. In this acrid wake, their faces expressionless, peasants strained over the pedals of heavily laden bicycles. Slung like great saddlebags over the rear wheel of each were two carefully packed baskets of privately grown vegetables. Once brought into the city, these peasant offerings were snapped up on city street corners by eager housewives, who disdained the flyblown mounds of bruised and crushed vegetables that lay limp and rotting in the state markets. The race to supply the tables of city folk was one that the peasants won handily, despite their transportation handicap, now that they were being allowed to compete with the state. I took out the first of the notebooks that I would fill on the journey and began to jot down my impressions in a jouncing hand.

"We're riding on the best highway in South China," Ming said with his secret smile as he saw me struggling to hold pen and notebook steady. "It is eighteen meters wide, has a total of four car lanes and two bike lanes, and it is paved. It's what is known in China as a Class One Highway." He glanced at me and his smile widened into a grin: "We won't see any roads as good as this in the back country."

Garden plot was giving way to rice paddy a few minutes later when we reached the turnoff for the main route westward, one that would take us up the course of the West River into the province of Kwangsi. "Class Three Highway," Ming reported. "Two lanes. Eight to nine meters wide. Paved." I quickly came to appreciate the quality of the road we had just left, for the going was rough, and Ming slowed from 50 to 30 m.p.h. As we continued at this unhurried pace, the road, which at first had scissored cleanly across the countryside, began to curve up and around a series of small rises and hollows. The landscape was shrugging off its alluvial flatness.

It felt good to be on the road. Toward the end of my lengthy stay in the congested Delta countryside I had occasionally come down with cabin fever, a benign form of claustrophobia that I had usually cured by evening drives into the commune seat to call on friends. Once or twice, when the hour was late, I simply set out on the circular road that linked the main villages of the commune, enjoying the cool night air and the sense of motion until I was brought round to my starting point. My current journey was driven by more purpose, but it generated the same pleasurable sense of freedom.

Still it seemed strange to be leaving the Pearl River Delta. During my months there I had grown fond of the languid beauty of that low-lying landscape, an intricate and enchanting natural mosaic of fresh-water ponds, mulberry patches, sugarcane stands, and garden plots. The only breaks in this lush panorama were made by occasional low, red hills, whose summits I had often sought on my walks. From this vantage point I could take in the whole: the village of grey-tiled brick homes close in on the hill's lower slopes, seeking the high ground against the times when the delta channels overflowed their dikes; the ponds luminous and lovely, adorning the earth below like strings of huge, liquid pearls; the embankments crowded with miniature forests of tiny mulberry trees, consigned to an arboreal dwarfdom by the various crops of silkworms that fed upon their leaves; the belts of tall, purple-stalked sugarcane that ran along the main dikes and canals. When a late summer evening wrapped the whole in a lucid haze, I could almost divine a tropical Eden.

Where we were now, the earth had a completely different aspect, one more typical of China south of the Yangtze River. The hills were higher and were often clumped together into ridges separated by meandering river valleys. Despite the more irregular relief of this hill-and-valley landscape, it had achieved a greater ecological coherence. The multifarious exploitation of the land for commerce had given way to the single-minded pursuit of subsistence. Instead of the blue and green parquet of fish ponds and market crops of the Delta, the lowlands here were a solid carpet of rice stalks, standing erect and emerald green in the June sun. Instead of a road crowded with vehicles hurrying to market, we saw only an occasional truck. More common were the grey-skinned water buffaloes that plodded lazily along the shoulder of the road, or basked in pools that fitted their great bodies as if made to measure. "Grain has replaced gain," I wrote of this ecological divide at the time, "and traction in the fields has become more important than transportation along the roads."

Still I observed that the basic patterns of peasant life persisted despite these economic differences. Here, as in the Delta, each village was a rabbit warren of houses tightly clustered about a few winding alleys and surrounded by a broad belt of fields. Here, too, the settlements hugged the hills, seeking the middle ground between flood and irrigation, safety and supply. The villages I was seeing had populations numbering in the hundreds rather than in the thousands as did Delta communities, but they were still as thickly scattered across the landscape as individual farmhouses were in Nebraska. Like Delta villages— or for that matter Nebraska farms—they were totally rural in character, places to live and work, not to buy and sell. Here, too, every bit of level land was under cultivation.

The intensity of cultivation and settlement was both triumph and curse. Many Western travelers, initially overwhelmed by the vast numbers of people who make their living off the land, see the Chinese peasant as engaged in a bitter and fatalistic struggle. One early description, not atypical, spoke of "a land gnawed to the subsoil by the ceaseless effort of innumerable generations, despoiled of all forest, cultivated to its last palm of earth, sapped of its vigor, yet where man is ever febrilely multiplying himself."[1] In the Delta I had been more impressed with the cheerful industry of a people who skillfully coaxed so much from the earth.

When the road curved close to one large, prosperous-looking village of one-story brick homes, I decided to take a closer look. The dirt track that led to the village was too narrow for the van to traverse safely, so I left Ming in the van and walked the hundred yards to the village, following the track as it wound around the single large pond, past a row of flanking lichee trees, and into the small clearing that the settlement fronted on. It was the custom in South China to take a siesta after the noonday meal, and most of the village was asleep. Only a few boys, brown as crickets, followed me as I circuited the alleyways. Curiosity kept their heads cocked sideways, but caution kept enough distance between themselves and the stranger so that they could ignore his questions. I walked out into the handkerchief-sized gardens that encircled the village—Canton's belt of truck gardens in miniature. These were the plots, averaging about the area of a one-car garage apiece, that the hundred-odd families in the village were allotted to grow vegetables for their own tables. By regulation this "self-till land" cannot exceed about 6 percent of the total acreage. The rest of the village land was one vast expanse of rice paddy, cut by an occasional irrigation ditch and further sectioned by low dikes of packed earth into large and regular fields. These were cultivated not by families but by production teams—the lowest level of the collective under the brigade and commune—that mobilized the labor of from fifteen to fifty peasant households.

Behind the village a long, low hill shouldered to the sky. Unlike the fertile paddy below, but like most of the hills we had passed, it was an ecological basket case. Centuries of villagers in search of wood for building and brush for kindling had reduced its once luxuriant tropical vegetation to a wasteland of coarse grass and ferns. The torrential sum-

[1] Quoted in George Cressey, *China's Geographic Foundations* (New York: McGraw-Hill, 1934), p. 355.

mer monsoon had sluiced away even this tenacious ground cover on the steeper slopes, leaving gullies of red ochre soil gaping open like running wounds. Except for a few patches of peanuts and sweet potatoes planted immediately behind the village and several rows of young orange trees that stood on one of the gentler lower slopes, the infertile earth of the hillside was left uncultivated. It would not repay the labor of clearing, planting, and irrigating—especially irrigating, which meant a back-breaking slog up ascending paths with water bucket and carrying pole.

Despite its ravaged appearance, the hill continued to figure impor-tantly in the life of the community it overshadowed. The barren hilltop served as a burial ground, and its heights were studded with omega-shaped graves old and new. From this hillside necropolis the ancestral spirits could look down on the living community below, keeping watch over their descendants as these performed the latest act of the ancient drama of production and reproduction that had been played out on these same acres for perhaps a thousand years.

From this vantage point, the ancestors would have observed no striking external changes following the coming of the Communists in 1949, even after the forced collectivization of the countryside in the fif-ties. The family land now belonged to the neighborhood production team, and the paddy fields would be larger and the garden plots smaller than the ancestors remembered. But they would have been relieved that their descendants continued to reside in the ancestral village, even if they referred to it as a production brigade, and were still making weekly visits to the same local market town, even if it was now called a com-mune. Those who had died more recently might resent how simply con-structed their graves were as compared with those of people who had died a generation earlier, but they would have been reassured by the sight of their families still eating, sleeping, loving, and fighting around the hearths that they had called home in their time. And all of the ancestors would have noted with satisfaction that the whole still formed the recognizable picture of rural life that the Chinese for centuries have called *tian, yuan, lu, mu,* or "fields, gardens, homes, and graves." It is in this intimate yet restricted setting, repeated many hundreds of thou-sands of times over the face of China, that 800 million Chinese peasants, nearly one-fifth of the world's population, were born, will live out their span of years, and will die, joining their ancestors in the cemetery that is always nearby.

"A modestly prosperous village. Well off for a rice-growing area." Ming offered this sober, straight-faced assessment when I got back in the van. But then he could not resist adding with a smile of condescension: "Not as wealthy as we in the Delta."

I nodded, for I too had seen the signs. By Western standards the Chinese countryside we were passing through was a morass of unrelieved destitution, but a year in a Chinese village had taught me the Chinese scale of rural well-being, sharpening my senses to the significance of the nuances of local economy, shelter, dress, and diet by which a rural community can be placed at a glance on a Chinese continuum of poverty and wealth. Although the village fronted a substantial expanse of paddy, the dirt road leading to it was unrutted, bespeaking the absence of farm machinery. Homes were built solidly enough, but their unplastered brick fronts and undecorated eaves lent them a sense of austerity, just as the clothing of the boys, though respectable enough, was of a slightly drabber hue, a slightly plainer cut, than those I was used to. Delta communities had been more or less affluent by Chinese standards. This village was merely on the upscale side of sufficiency. "Let's be off," I said to Ming, thinking about what lay downscale.

The road made a great loop southwards, bringing the West River into view for the first time before swinging away again to come upon the North River a few miles upstream from the confluence of these two arteries. The West River was the larger, but the North River was a formidable swath of blue water in its own right, and I was surprised to find that it was not spanned by a bridge. Instead, like most rivers in China, it could be forded only by ferryboat. The pair of ferries in service here, at Stable Crossing as it was called, could handle only a dozen vehicles each trip, and heavy trucks were queued up for a half mile before the loading ramp. Most of these trucks had left Canton at dawn for the city of Chaoch'ing across the river, and Ming avowed that it would be nightfall before those at the tail end of the line would make the opposite shore. As a passenger vehicle we had priority, and we pulled past the frozen file of trucks to join the much shorter caravan of buses and vans at the top of the dike near the ferry ramp. Even so, we faced a half-an-hour wait and a passage of equal duration before we would be on our way. It seemed to me a real transportation bottleneck for such an important east-west route, but I told myself that the line of low bridge piers rising from the river a little ways downstream meant that this obstacle would be eliminated in a year or so.

"When will the bridge be completed?" I innocently asked a driver standing nearby.

He looked at me and laughed, a short, contemptuous, yapping sound devoid of mirth. "It was planned to be a steel bridge for trains and motor vehicles," he began. "Like the one built in 1958 over the Yangtze River at Wuhan. But the project had to be given up for lack of funds and materials. That was ten years ago." He paused and smiled Ming's secret smile. "Who knows when it will be completed."

The great bridge over the Yangtze River at Wuhan had been completed in a frenzy of construction in 1958 at the beginning of the Great Leap Forward. It strode boldly across the mile-wide river on eight great piers, a huge structure of three levels: train tracks, a roadway, and a walkway. It had been at once a testimony to the power of the newborn people's state, a slap in the face of foreign engineers who said that it couldn't be built, and a symbol of national pride. It had also, apparently, been a goad for provincial administrations to set about building their own "impossible" bridges.

I looked again at the unfinished bridge, seeing it in a different light. There was no sight of activity anywhere along its length or approaches. The meager resources of a province had proved unequal to the task it had here undertaken. The piers had been abandoned in the stream, inadvertent monuments to poor planning and public waste, stepping-stones to nowhere.

At the top of the dike an old woman was hawking glasses of tepid, murky-looking tea to the drivers from a flat-topped wooden cart little bigger than a toy wagon, while a few yards away a little girl wearing a bamboo hat the size of a sombrero had set up shop on top of a bamboo basket selling unshelled peanuts and dried salted plums. Ming warned me away from the tea, but said that the peanuts would be all right, so I walked over to the second stand. The proprietress, a tiny wren of a child who scarely came up to my waist, looked successively awed, embarrassed, and ready to take flight as I approached. But she held her ground, probably stopped by the thought of abandoning her wares to this odd-looking stranger. "Ten fen," she managed to chirp when I asked her how much a lid of peanuts were, and as I pulled a ten fen[2] note from my pocket and handed it to her, she even risked a cocked glance at me from under the brim of her enormous hat. I smiled reassuringly at her and started to reach for my peanuts, but she snatched the lid away. "Hold out your hand," she told me shyly, and poured the dozen peanuts into my cupped palm. The lid, cut out of the bottom of a tin can, was not part of the bargain.

With the ten-fen note safely squirreled away in the glass jar that served as her cashbox, and the rescued lid refilled with peanuts from a little sack, she seemed to relax a little, and I gently tried to draw her out. She sold several yuan of peanuts and dried plums every day, she told me, and cleared about fifty fen, or about as much as her father made working in the collective fields. She claimed to be twelve, but that meant that she was actually eleven, or maybe only ten, in Western years for the Chinese reckon themselves to be one year old at birth and have a birthday every Chinese New Years thereafter. A Chinese baby can turn two years old on the second day of its life if it happens to be born on the eve of Chinese New Years. But whether ten or eleven, in the Delta the girl would still be attending primary school. Here, she had stopped school a year ago after completing fourth grade, and had been selling peanuts at this crossing since.

The ferry that we would be taking swung in on its final approach. Diesel engines lugged down as screws reversed direction, frantically clutching at the frothing water, taking off way. A little too slowly, I thought as the ferry banged home into the slip with a cacaphony of groaning wood and grinding metal. The noise roused Ming from the sleep that he was able to fall into at a moment's notice (a skill that he claimed to have honed to perfection in the military), and he started the van. I stood off to the side, waiting as the flagman off-loaded the arriving vehicles. Nearby I noticed a middle-aged peasant man with a mattock working what I first took to be dark river mud into carrying pole hods. "Not fertilizer, fuel," he corrected me gruffly when I asked. A coal truck had overturned here two days ago while coming down the steep

---

[2] There are 100 fen in one yuan, which is worth about fifty cents.

landing ramp. The chunks of coal had been quickly gathered up by
scavenging villagers, leaving only a dark slash in the mud. But he was
hoping that there was enough coal dust mixed in with the mud so that,
with a little straw and a few days of sun, it would burn. "Kindling is
scarce here," he grunted. Overturning trucks, on the other hand, must
be common, I thought, watching anxiously as Ming gunned the van up
onto the landing ramp of the ferry, which was slowly being twisted away
from the slip by the current.

After the river crossing, the road gradually worked itself back
southward to the West River, coming upon it just above the Lingyang
Gorge, which pinches the river into a narrow, undulating channel
roughly 250 feet wide and deep. Here on the north bank sat the city of
Chao-ch'ing ("Establish-Fortune"), a Chinese Vicksburg, command-
ing the river route to Canton. It was a function it had been performing
for millennia. Dynastic records show that Chao-ch'ing is an ancient
city, founded a century before the birth of Christ, and that it even served
as the capital of the entire province during the Ming dynasty
(1368–1644). But for all I could see from a slow turn across town that
day, it might have been founded in the last few decades. Or maybe
thrown up would be a better word. Everywhere the single, stolid mode
of China's socialist architecture held sway: ugly, squat, hastily constructed boxes of brick and concrete, varying only in size. A few structures, it was true, were painted the drab yellow favored for official
buildings. But most—the factories, the offices, and the long rows of two-
story housing blocks—had been left a pockmarked grey. Even among
buildings newly rising, each enveloped in a web of bamboo scaffolding
that looked scarcely sturdy enough to support the men who clambered
spider-like over it, there were no exceptions to this dead practicality of
expression. The city was afflicted with an instant aging that no frenzy
of construction could cure. Chao-ch'ing reminded me of the mill towns
of nineteenth-century Lancashire: early industrial revolution.

A last row of dormitories and we reemerged into the park-like countryside. It almost seemed to me that there were two Chinas, the one a
mechanical society of belching factories and grimy machines, the other
an organic sanctuary of checkered fields and peasant handicrafts; the
one anachronistic, the other timeless.

For the first time since leaving the Delta, I found myself facing a dirt road. "Class Four Highway," Ming, who had been silent in the city, sang out. "Five to seven yards wide. Unpaved dirt over rock. Not very comfortable going but passable in most weather. This is the kind of road we'll be on from now on." And then with a cheerful grimace: "This is what China's main highway system connecting the provinces is like."

So I noted in my journal, adding in quizzical parentheses: "The worse conditions grow, the happier Ming seems to become."

As for me, I was increasingly possessed by an eerie sense that we had somehow taken a turn in time rather than space and driven into another era. The heavy, Russian-model trucks with which we had shared the road to Chao-ch'ing had disappeared. Roadside villages were dominated for the most part by an ancestral hall in the traditional style, its ridgepole and eaves decorated with squared, patterned ornaments that could have been copied from the archaic metalwork of the Eastern Chou dynasty (771–221 B.C.). No matter that the ancestral tablets within had probably been burned in the Great Leap Forward, and that the building itself now served as office and storeroom of the village collective; the rustic whole offered up to our passing eyes only a few drooping strands of electric wire and an occasional parked bicycle as evidence that it inhabited the present century.

For the next twenty miles the road clung to the West River like a shy child its mother. We were never out of sight of its swift green flow. Of all China's rivers, only the mighty Yangtze carries more water to the sea. We passed an upbound riverboat, one of the steel-hulled two-hundred-footers that make regular passenger runs between Chiangmen at the river's mouth and the city of Wuchow 170 miles upstream. I watched the boat smoothly plow its way up the middle of the big river, its wake rippling out to mark the arrow of its progress, momentarily wishing that I was on board instead of pounding up and down the bluffs alongside.

The road had become a thing to wrench a snake's back. It seemed just a matter of time before the van would be rattled back into its component parts. Ming had dropped down to about twenty-five miles an hour when we hit dirt and was now forced to go even slower. Inclines were the worst. Here rains had washed the road's loose topsoil away, slucing out the ruts into snaking gullies, exposing the rocks below. As we jolted up one slope I heard the sudden sound of breaking glass. ''There goes our water supply,'' Ming grimaced. Our two thermos bottles full of boiled water had shattered.

As if in propitiation for our loss, Ming began to talk of rural roads, how they are built and, for better or worse, maintained. Construction begins with the trenching of the future road. Then successive layers of smaller and smaller stones are laid, the interstices being filled with soil. Finally, the whole is topped with a layer of cushioning dirt.

Protecting this thin layer of arterial topsoil against the ravages of transiting trucks and passing rainstorms is the central task of Chinese road maintenance crews. A more thankless occupation can hardly be imagined. During the dry season the wheels of passing vehicles fling the dirt up to the center and shoulders of the road; day after day, road workers wielding long-handled twig brooms patiently sweep it back down into the ruts. During the rainy season huge swathes of soil wash away entirely; after each storm workers bring in new fill by wheelbarrow and handcart, using shovels to spread it out and tamp it down where the underlying rock has been exposed.

Like so much in China, almost all of this sweeping, hauling, and shoveling is done by hand. Only twice—both times in the vicinity of a city—did I see crews aided by animal power: a water buffalo harnessed to a diagonal wooden scraper that it dragged slowly along the road. These bovine road graders were intended, like the brooms, to move the displaced dirt back into the ruts. The road surface was so uneven, though, that the scraper bounced roughly along and left the dirt standing in little diagonal rows. The brooms worked better. Notwithstanding its limited road system, there must be more street sweepers in China than in the rest of the world combined.

The road sweepers live and work out of isolated little road houses called ''road maintenance stations'' that are run by the Ministry of Transportation. The stations are roughly ten miles apart along the main interprovincial arteries, which means that by the standards of rural China they are within easy walking—and sweeping—distance of one another. Officially classified as workers, sweepers are paid salaries and receive state rice rations. But they bring up the tail end of this favored class, trailing even Chinese garbage collectors, who as Ming pointed out at least get to live in the cities. Their dirty, demanding jobs, their permanent assignment to rural areas, often far from any sizeable center of population, make road sweepers unattractive marriage choices. To make a match, many of them have to turn to the only caste that ranks lower than they do—the peasantry.

"It can't be that bad," I objected after Ming finished. "At least they get to live in the countryside."

"Worst job under heaven," Ming countered firmly. "All their life in the sun and the dirt just like peasants."

It helped to have Ming along to strike a cautionary note, I reflected. The waste of human potential inherent in sending bright young men and women to sweep roads or do stoop labor should be self-evident. But there is a cloying temptation on the part of Westerners—I was feeling its tug myself—to presume the contentment of rural Chinese from the rustic serenity and natural beauty of their surroundings. Ming was close enough to peasant life to see it for what it was.

The road finally curled away from the river at a town called Lupu, carrying us up a narrow valley carved out by a tiny tributary. The sense of snug prosperity that had characterized West River villages, benefiting both from paddy on the near level flood plain of the river and riverine commerce, ebbed quickly away. Settlements and their surrounding paddy shrank in tandem, while the hills that rose behind them grew ever more imposing, their bases now in terraced rice paddy, their tops crowned with a lush natural vegetation. Nature was reclaiming the landscape, making life more difficult for Chinese men and women.

A rice paddy is not just the South Chinese peasant's central obsession. It is his only one. Rice is the high-status food of Chinese culture, and a paddy produces more than twice as many pounds of staple food per acre as dry land crops like corn and sweet potatoes. A village's prosperity can be taken in at a glance by the extent of the paddy that it fronts, and no village without a paddy, unless it is near a city, can be prosperous. It is not a Chinese peasant's home but his rice paddy that is his most valuable possession, and it is for the gift of paddy, more than anything else, that he gratefully remembers and honors his ancestors.

Transforming dry land to wet paddy can be as easy as building mud dikes and diverting a stream through the enclosure thus created, if the terrain cooperates. But in these parts nature had upped the stakes. The land had to be leveled and walled in stretches before it would hold the water required by rice seedlings, work that done by hoe and carry-ing pole is nasty, brutish, and interminable. The terraced fields that wound so gracefully around the lower reaches of the hills—forming a contour map in 3-D—had been carved out at a cost of hundreds of man-years of backbreaking labor.

A cluster of dwellings came into sight ahead on the left, whose tawny color caught my eye. Up to this point the villages had presented a near-solid phalanx of red brick. But in this community, though the homes were well laid out, with dark red tile roofs and gabled facades, and two were even whitewashed, they were one and all built of a pale adobe. Perhaps the land was gradually losing its alluvial richness, I thought as we drew near, or perhaps the ratio of paddy to population had dropped below some critical level. This thought was checked as a brick kiln came into view.

The contrast between the village of mud bricks on the left hand side of the road and the brick kiln on the right added a new dimension to the puzzle. Brick kilns run by collectives abound in the Delta, but the collec-tives fire bricks first of all for the use of their own members. Maybe this was a minority group that used adobe by custom. I motioned Ming to pull over.

There were half-a-dozen men around the kiln, stripped down to undershirts in the early afternoon heat, feeding kindling into the several mouths of the furnace. The men broke off from their work to stare amiably at me as I disembarked.

"Firing bricks to build homes?" I casually asked the men in Can-tonese, handing out cigarettes all around. I don't smoke, but I had found that Chinese peasants, almost to a man, do. I always carried a pack of cigarettes with me to offer new acquaintances, a pungent Hong Kong brand that the peasants invariably praised after their stale, coarse cuts.

The men smiled uncertainly at one another for a second before an older man, obviously in charge, took it upon himself to speak. "Not for homes," he said. "We sell them to the city of Chao-ch'ing." He spoke in a Cantonese more clipped than I had been used to hearing, and some of the words came out off-tone, but it was clear that this was a band of Cantonese, not Hakka, Hunanese, or some non-Han minority.

"Must get sixty inches of rain here a year," I offered. "Mud bricks don't last long in this kind of climate."

"Can't be helped. We can't afford to buy them ourselves. Fuel's too dear." He began to lay out the economics of brick production as the other men concentrated on their cigarettes, taking long drags and holding the smoke in their lungs as if they expected a high.

The kindling required to fire the bricks was painstakingly collected by two dozen villagers who daily fanned out over the surrounding hills in search of dead brushwood. They received one yuan per hundred catties, an amount that it took several days to gather. Nearly 600 yuan of kindling—50,000 to 60,000 catties—had to be burned to produce one load of 27,000 bricks. The labor that went into the bricks themselves added another 300 yuan. The clay soil had to be dug up, carted back to the kiln, mixed with water, screened through a mesh to remove stones, formed in wooden molds, set out to dry in the sun, stacked inside the kiln, and tended for the ten days of firing. Then there was the cost of transporting the bricks by river barge down to the city of Chao-ch'ing— about 100 yuan. After culling, a kiln's worth of bricks, selling for 5 yuan per hundred, would bring about 1,300 yuan. The brigade made a profit of 300 to 350 yuan each firing, but it was a profit permitted only by extremely depressed wages. The men at the kiln earned only 40 fen a day. The peasants combing the hills for brushwood earned even less.

The kiln was important, my guide explained. With the money it brought in, the brigade had bought an electric motor and pump from a state factory two years ago, and a walking tractor—a kind of oversized Rototiller—this year. Were the brigade's 150 families to divide the bricks up among themselves, they would have no way of buying these things.

This was it in a nutshell. No matter the enormous amount of manual labor that it siphoned away from farming, the brick kiln, I now realized, represented this community's economic lifeline to the larger Chinese world. Without it, they would forego their most important means of participating, however marginally, in the larger cash economy, and would be thrown back primarily on their local peasant economy of barter and exchange. With it, they were in a position to gradually free themselves from their hand-to-mouth existence. Adobe homes or no, I was soon to find that these villagers should be counted among the fortunate.

After a quick meal of canned milk and crackers, we drove on. The afternoon passed in a panorama of adobe villages, each rooted naturally in its timeless garden setting, paddy below, hill above. It is as if each hollow had always been home to the three-score families that pass their lives there now. In most countries this is a pleasant illusion of the traveler, who transits too quickly to see change, and who prefers to imagine a reassuring stability containing and cushioning his own reckless rush through the world. Yet in China these instincts happen, ironically, to be right. I stopped at a village called Wang's Hamlet, and was told by an ancient wreck whose eyes were milky with cataracts that the Wang in question was his great-grandfather sixteen times removed. Although the main body of Wangs had remained here, near the grave of the first ancestor, over the centuries a few of the more adventurous or less favored Wangs had left this hollow for other hollows in other hills. But even this trickle had been staunched by the population registration law of 1958, which legally bound the Wangs to the patch of earth that their ancestor staked a claim to so many centuries ago. The community had been caught like a fly in amber, a perfectly preserved specimen, rare outside of China, of the Traditional Village. Wang's Hamlet was a self-contained, self-sufficient, and self-reproducing colony of human beings, with the young, the middle-aged, and the old in perfect demographic proportions. In a world of jet travel and communications satellites, the village seemed as unnatural in its manmade isolation as a colony of flour beetles grown in a laboratory flask.

Shortly before dark we passed through the commune of Le-ch'eng. Its name translates as "Happy City," an advertisement that commune life must have a hard time living up to. Chinese place names are for the most part pleasingly literal. The Han explorer who christened the West, North, and East Rivers was simply stating a fact. Not that all natural features are equally immutable. Big Oak Village was named after its most prominent feature. The tree was felled by lightning but the name stands. Chen's Village is home to a mixed bag of surnames, none of whom are the grandsons of Chen.

At 8:00 P.M. we stopped to refuel at Wu-lung, a quiet commune town whose name, "Armed Embankments," suggested that things had been more lively here in the past. As the gas from the first of our three 50-liter cans ran down the siphon hose into the tank below, we talked about where to spend the night. Ming instantly vetoed my idea of sleeping in the van. "Too dangerous," he said with a smile. "Drivers never sleep in their vehicles unless they have no other choice. They are afraid of roving gangs of bandits.'' We decided to press on to the next county seat shown on my map, the West River port town of Te-ch'ing (''Celebration of Virtue''), twenty-five miles away. From there it would be a straight shot up the river to the city of Wuchow, the gateway to the heartland province of Kwangsi.

The twilight turned the hills into black, humpbacked dragons that devoured the nesting villages only to be swallowed up in their turn by the larger darkness of the sky. There was something oppressive in the thought of the silent, huddled masses of humanity that I knew we were continuously passing. While the road made a point of bisecting county towns and passed through the occasional commune seat, it did not stoop to serve villages, and these had vanished into the night leaving nothing except an endless ribbon of dirt fringed with saw grass. For all we could see, we might have been traveling through a wasteland. There were no gas stations, no truck stops, no warehouses, no stacks of wood or goods awaiting shipment, no tiny stands selling bananas or pomelos, no shops for hungry travelers offering dumplings or noodles, and no homes. The road demanded right-of-way from the land but gave nothing in return. Under the Ministry of Transportation's five-year plan, an item: Connect all provinces with Class Four Roads. It was done, child's play for the central planners of a totalitarian regime, but it had not brought prosperity in its wake. The occasional driver who barreled his truck along the road was intent on some distant city, and stopped only to relieve himself or make emergency repairs. The peasants who walked along the road to market twice a week would have been just as well served by the footpath that had once run here.

It was nearly ten o'clock when the dim glow of a handful of streetlights beckoned out of the darkness. The dirt road graduated to concrete with a thump, and flat-topped buildings, so unlike gracefully roofed peasant homes, closed in on both sides. We had reentered the magic circle of paved roads and streetlights that sets urban China apart from the countryside. Streetlights and pavement might have been officially decreed for county-level and higher capitals by the Peking Ministry of Transportation (or the Ministry of Public Security), so faithfully was this rule observed. None of the communes—not to mention villages—I visited were favored with these amenities, while none of the county towns I drove through were without them.

Directly beneath the first streetlight, a state-run noodle shop was still open despite the late hour. Like most rural noodle shops and teahouses, it was medieval, with packed earth floors, moist brick walls, and rough wooden tables, round after the Chinese fashion and surrounded by three-legged stools. The tables numbered six, and nothing short of a jack-plane could have removed the encrusted impurities from their tops. Only one of the tables was occupied—by drivers, to judge from the truck parked outside, like ourselves late on the road.

We ordered two bowls of wontons—along with rice and wheat noodles, the only items on the menu—from a surly-faced waiter, whose only sign of having heard our order was his abrupt departure into the kitchen. "And a dish of garlic," Ming shouted after his retreating back.

As we started in on our wontons, Ming picked up a fresh garlic, peeled it, and popped it into his mouth. Then he pushed the dish over to me. "You'd better eat a few cloves too," he said, smiling wryly. "It's a trick that we drivers use to avoid stomach trouble. Garlic is an antiseptic. These little noodle shops are filthy. They don't understand a thing about hygiene. Look at your bowl."

There were several patches of light-grey grease around the edges of the bowl, and a glance at the underside revealed a grimy greenish scum. The bowl had not been washed prior to use. Perhaps it had not even been rinsed. I took Ming's advice, matching him clove for clove. We finished the garlic well before the wontons.

The waiter, loosening up a little as we paid the bill cum tip, gave us directions to a county-run "reception center," a kind of hostel mostly used by cadres traveling on official business. Cadres can afford the 2.50 yuan charge per person and can present a valid travel permit. Few others can. At the center, we were given a 10 × 25 foot room containing three single beds draped with mosquito nets and a small table on which sat two thermos bottles of hot water. "Use hot water sparingly," the young attendant cautioned us. The wood-burning stove that supplied the center's hot water was lit only once a day, and there would be no hot water until noon tomorrow. We took a quick shower of cold water—the center did have running water—and then crawled under the mosquito nets.

In the summer in China you court rheumatism by sleeping under a fan or insomnia by trying to sleep without it. Here I was spared this

Hobson's choice: The room had no fan. The night was hot and sultry, made worse by the thick cotton nets, which kept out not only their intended attackers, but any stray tendrils of air as well. Despite my tiredness, for it had been a grueling day, I was unable to doze off in the enervating heat.

I got out my map and began to measure off distances. It seemed to me that my journey had already taken me across half the breadth of China, but by the map I was only a little more than one hundred miles from Canton, though the van's odometer had rolled off about twice that distance. The primitive, twisting roads made a nonsense of distance.

Then again, I reminded myself, I was traveling to take in the countryside, not simply to transit it. Leave to tourists the jet planes and trains. I preferred the leisurely gait of my van. The slowness of our passing was a virtue. Holding this thought, I fell into a dreamless sleep.

CHAPTER TWO

Up the West River

THE town of Te-ch'ing was much less appealing in the bright morning sunlight than it had been as a beckoning of street lights. It was little more than a tic-tac-toe of streets, a few simple squares of drab, washed-out-looking buildings. The noodle shop of the previous night had not yet opened, but the town's other diner was doing a brisk business in rice congee. Despite my fondness for Chinese food—I had eaten nothing else for a year—this is one dish that I pass by whenever possible. It consists of white rice, and nothing but white rice, boiled into a bland, starchy, sticky pap. It has always reminded me of kindergarten paste, except that it has even less flavor. On this morning I finished a bowl anyway, figuring that it might be a long time until lunch. Ming had three, slurping the congee from his rice bowl with the enthusiasm of an American attacking his ham and eggs.

Then we took to the road, traveling, as always, up the West River. This had been the path the early Han Chinese settlers had followed. Chinese armies had come first to Kwangtung and Kwangsi, areas then occupied by the hostile Yueh, during the Han dynasty (200 B.C. to 220 A.D.). Military colonization had followed, with settlements founded at strategic points along the West River and its main tributaries by soldiers who were encouraged to start families and engage in agriculture. With pacification, traders had followed, settling in and around the existing colonies to trade with the soldiers and the surrounding tribes. Following many centuries of political and cultural influence, the Delta and coastal regions were settled first by Han Chinese, during the Tang and Sung dynasties. Later, during the Ming dynasty, drawn by the promise of lush, low-lying valleys in which they could grow their prized rice crops, the descendants of these early Cantonese settlers began to move inland, always heading upriver. Thus the bulk of the Han Chinese in Kwangsi even today speak Cantonese.

The West River soon narrowed between high, irregular bluffs, and the road turned away, seeking easier ground up a small tributary. This valley it had carved between hills was a narrow one, leaving no room for rice paddy. The slopes were mostly planted in sugarcane, though there were also occasional groves of slender, arching bamboo, wafting in the air as gracefully as a solitary flute playing at night. Here the villages edged the road, for there was no other level ground on which to build, and the houses stood open to inspection. I picked a house at random and stopped to note particulars:

The house has no frills, no facade, no gables. It is a simple structure of naked adobe. But it is built solidly, a log cabin in mud brick, and has a tile roof. The adobe bricks are fresh, only a year or two old. The windows are high and small, the wooden door thick and bolted from the inside, suggesting that in this part of the countryside, these precautions against local bandits are still necessary. (In the Delta only older homes still have these high, narrow, burglarproof windows—"cat windows" they are called, because only a cat could possibly gain entry through them.) An old quern—a stone mill of the kind turned by hand—stands upright in the front yard, its two polished granite stones still used to crush rice into flour. Is there no electric mill nearby?

An old man with a face worn by the toil of years emerged from behind the house, laden down with carrying pole and two buckets. His stringy muscles, wound over his bones like copper wire over an armature, moved tautly as he walked. Like all carrying polers, he gave the impression that he was balancing on a narrow, invisible beam. "What's this place called, uncle?" I asked as he neared the road.

His eyes darted at me from under grizzled brows. He slowly stopped his forward motion and set down his burden, his face slack with the effort. "Shan-tsui," he wheezed, slightly out of breath. "Mouth of the Mountains."

"Pretty small team," I offered. I could count about a dozen homes scattered across the gentle slope, some partly hidden by clumps of bamboo.

"Big enough for this poor place," he replied. "There are twenty-three families in the team and one hundred members in all."

"How much you get for a day's work here?"

"Fifty fen," he replied. "Highest in the brigade. Most teams only get thirty fen. Over in the hills"—added in a tone of voice that suggested that it was the outer darkness—"they get only twenty fen a day."

"Any hand tractors?"

"Nope," he replied, "But in our team nearly every family has a bike." His manner suggested that this was unusual locally, although in the Delta every family had a bike, and many had two.

I watched the old man carefully get back under his burden, his tendons moving like plucked guitar strings, and walk away in short, wire-drawn steps. I wondered that someone so elderly should be pressed into such heavy service. In the Delta he would be spending his days relaxing in the company of cronies.

I had seen few bikes in the village, but rounding a curve not far down the road we came upon five cyclists. They were riding abreast, in a kind of calvary formation, and there was no way around. Ming belatedly slammed on the brakes. We slid through the dirt toward them and I saw that we would hit at least one and possibly two. I braced myself for the impact of metal on flesh and bone. At the last possible moment the formation parted smoothly, two to the left, three to the right, and we were safely by them. The near miss didn't seem to have taught them anything. I looked around to see them still five abreast, ready for their next game of calvary charge chicken.

"If you hit someone in China, you'd better kill them," Ming said with an edge of irony in his voice, seemingly unaffected by our near miss. "Otherwise you could wind up paying for the rest of your life. A driver who cripples someone must support him. That means fifty yuan or more a month. If you kill someone things are much simpler. There is a one-time payment of about two thousand yuan to the family of the victim. Drivers sometimes back over their victims after an accident to make sure that they are quite dead.'' He paused to let this sink in and then added, altogether too cheerfully given the lugubriousness of his topic: ''Human life is cheap in China.''

I was quite sure that most rural Chinese were totally ignorant of this homocidal tendency on the part of truck drivers. For one thing, they walked (or cycled) on any part of the road they pleased: right, left, or dead center. For another, they showed a total, and under the circumstances, foolhardy, absence of fear, giving way to oncoming trucks only at the last moment, and turning aside for overtaking ones only after a series of earsplitting blasts on the horn. The average peasant in the interior has about half as much traffic sense as a Rhode Island Red.

I would like to say that Ming, for his part, took the possibility of these fatal and ruinous encounters to heart, but he appeared not to. Rather, he seemed to cherish a belief that all bicyclists and pedestrians were nothing but mirages that would dissolve if approached closely enough. He used his brakes only as a last resort and then only when collision seemed a foregone conclusion. Only our slow rate of advance kept us from annihilating a large number of the rural population in the course of our journey.

All things considered, it did not surprise me to read later in the *Kwang Ming Daily* that China led the world in traffic fatalities, with 36 deaths per 100 million kilometers traveled. In America only 2.1 people die over the same distance.

The road returned to the West River at a place called Fengchow, which means ''blockaded island,'' an appropriate name for an old river city built on a channel island. Fengchow had once been a bustling center of river trade, and the downriver half of the three-mile-long island was crowded with the warehouses and wharves that had once belonged to Cantonese merchants. But as we drew nearer I saw that few boats were tied up along the sagging wharves, and the buildings seemed in sad repair. Ming said that the river trade had dropped off after the shipping companies were expropriated in the fifties. Not only did the bureaucrats assigned to manage them lack commercial experience, but as communists they had an active bias against acquiring it. Better not to buy and sell at all than run the risk of buying and selling at a profit.

The road had improved following its return to the river, and shortly after we passed Fengchow it became a ribbon of macadam stretching off into the distance. It was a pattern I had seen repeatedly during my stay in China, even on the thirty-minute trip from my Delta village into the commune seat. Near the village the road was little more than a pastiche of potholes, hardly traversable at all after a rain. The next section, part of the main road linking the commune to the county seat, was better maintained, and the strip immediately in front of the commune head-quarters had even been paved in concrete. In China paving was a mea-sure of the radius of power and privilege, and I knew that we would soon be in Wuchow.

The beginning of this Third Class Highway brought into view the first traffic sign I had seen since leaving Canton. It was a crude line drawing of a bridled horse's head on a yellow background inside a heavy red border. I didn't need Ming to tell me that this lightly traveled road was for some reason off-limits to the horse, donkey, and water buffalo carts of the local peasantry. With suburban buses few in number, and the price of tickets beyond the means of most peasants, this prohibition meant that rural Chinese must walk or ride bicycles (if they have them) on trips into the city.

Later, in an old geography of China by George Cressey, I came across an intriguing passage that helped me make sense of the current ban. It read: "[Wuchow] city authorities have passed an ordinance pro-hibiting rickshaws and man-pulled carts, in the hope of passing directly to the automobile age."[1] To judge from the traffic on Wuchow's streets, in which pedestrians and cyclists vastly outnumbered motor vehicles, the banning of rickshaws around 1930 did not lead people to buy cars in large numbers. The move did accomplish something, however. Like the current prohibition of the carts of the peasants, it rid the city's streets of another kind of "feudal" conveyance.

Cressey also wrote admiringly about the "recently widened streets and new business buildings in the model city of Wuchow." I can only wonder at what the city must have been like before these early doses of urban planning. The Wuchow I saw was a maze of narrow, winding streets tightly packed with two-story buildings that had once been the shops and trading concerns of Cantonese merchants but now served as

[1] George Cressey, *China's Geographic Foundations* (New York: McGraw-Hill, 1934), p. 367.

state offices and dormitories. To be fair, there was little that could be done, for the city was built at the confluence of the West River and its northern tributary, the Kwei ("Cinnamon") River, on land that made San Francisco look like an airport runway.

The streets all wound down to the rivers, on which rows of rickety wooden piers gave berth to Chinese junks of all sizes, from hundred-foot river barges to ten-foot sampans. The barges had regular crews but the sampans were family affairs, home to boat people who ate, slept, worked, and played out their lives on these tiny craft. According to Ming, even the smallest boats were owned by the state, which took its rent in the form of quotas of fish to catch and goods to haul.

Few of Wuchow's residents remember the colonies of British and German traders who lived in that city in the years between 1897, when it was opened as a treaty port under an article of the Burmese Frontier Convention, and 1949, when the Communists closed it to foreign trade. Almost no foreigners have been allowed to visit Wuchow since that time, despite its size (estimated population 200,000) and proximity to Hong Kong. These are the conclusions I came to after a solitary stroll up a side street ended ten minutes later with me hurrying along in the vanguard of a procession of hundreds. I had taken no pictures, engaged in no conversations, done nothing to attract attention to myself, but still the restless people of Wuchow had clamped on to me like piranhas attacking a wounded deer. Had it been evening, when students and young workers hit the streets hungry for a little action, I would have been prey for the eyes of thousands. As it was, I climbed back aboard the van with the relief of a runner reaching home plate. Nowhere in the world is a foreigner more of a spectacle than on the streets of China's inland cities.

This experience never happened to me in the towns I passed through, even when it was market day, and the streets were filled with people. I was stared at but not hounded, and if I was followed at all, it was by a small group of subdued young men who kept their distance. This was even more true in the villages, whose residents were content to watch warily from their doorsteps. I have seen groups of peasants scatter before my approach as half-wild creatures would before an annoying interloper who tried to pet them. Even when they held their ground, they often were abashed and ill-at-ease, heads down and toes scuffing the dirt. It is only the city dwellers who, secure in their privileges, aggressive in their numbers, and parochial in their isolation from the rest of the world, treat foreigners as a circus sideshow.

We stopped at a state-run truck stop on the outskirts of the city for lunch. It was our first real meal since leaving Canton, and we dug hungrily into the huge, greasy mounds of fried rice that were set down before us. I was relieved to see that this time, satisfied with the level of hygiene observed, Ming skipped the garlic. We finished up with a few bottles of stout from the local Wuchow brewery, and drank a toast to the long-departed Germans. We did not tarry, though, for we wanted to make Kweilin by nightfall.

The paved road continued to unroll before us, even though we had left the city behind. I was mildly surprised about this, and even more so after a glance at the map revealed that there was not a single town of any consequence for the next fifty miles. I somewhat uneasily wondered aloud if this expensive ribbon of asphalt didn't lead to a military base. Ming said that an ordinary encampment would hardly rate such a road, and instead ventured that it was some kind of high-priority secret installation. Ten miles later we found out that Ming's guess had been closer to the mark.

Into view came a large complex of buildings, the size and elegance of whose construction made it clear even from a distance that this was no ordinary village. As we drove nearer, I realized that even the *binguan,* the "guest palaces" for foreigners, could not compare with the clusters of dacha-like structures scattered over perhaps two hundred landscaped acres of grass, trees, and shrubbery that I was seeing. With its two-story, semi-attached buildings of brilliant white topped by smartly angled roofs of dark red tile standing in staggered rows, the grouping looked for all the world like a Santa Monica condominium complex. I have seen nothing like it in China either before or since. A wiry peasant in tattered blue whom I questioned a little further up the road confirmed what I had already guessed, that this was a resort run by the prefecture for the local Communist gentry.

The county "reception center" where we had stayed in Te-ch'ing was but the lowest-ranking of a whole array of resort communities. Not only the central government but also provincial, municipal, and prefectural authorities operate such resorts for the local political elite and visiting dignitaries. I had heard that a number of provincial party committees had built exclusive resorts that rivaled the central government's

Beihaihe, an enclave on the Bohai Gulf about 165 miles west of Peking, in luxury. Now I knew that even prefectural resorts, secluded somewhere within the dozen-odd counties that make up such units, could be impressive. Taken in the context of the real villages that so thickly dotted these worn, brown hills, this play village of the elite seemed to shine altogether too brightly, providing a rather too obvious allegory of communism, Animal Farm–style.

A few yards after we had passed the guarded entrance of this resort, I was brought abruptly back to the realities of Chinese rural life when the road turned irretrievably to dirt. What followed was the worst-maintained stretch of road we had yet encountered, and the van groaned and rattled in protest as we picked our way along. Ming said with his secret smile that the upkeep of the mandarin highway we had just left probably took most of the meager funds that the local transportation office had available.

The road left the valley of the Cinnamon River and began cutting and twisting through the rugged, mountainous territory that lay to the west. This was Kwangsi proper, an isolated and barren province known above all for its extreme poverty and persistent lawlessness. Except for a few areas near its eastern border with Kwangtung and its northern border with Hunan, it is a province that has never known prosperity. Banditry and other forms of unrest were endemic to the province, and occasionally spilled over its borders. The Taiping Rebellion in the 1850s, a bloody civil war that doomed China's imperial tradition, was spearheaded by armies of Kwangsi malcontents. The Red Seventh Army—formed in 1929 and led by Teng Hsiao-p'ing, then a young man in his mid-twenties—was made up of Kwangsi recruits.

The backwoods area we were passing through must have had a name, but the only set of maps I had been able to purchase before setting out on my trip didn't show any. This was the *China Map Handbook,* published by the government, and it had been a great disappointment. It provided a sketch of urban destinations, showing only the cities and major towns of each province, along with the railroads, rivers, and roads that linked them. I was interested in the countryside, but on these maps the Kwangsi countryside was an unmarked void, a no-man's-land. Perhaps the official mapmakers couldn't imagine that anyone would want to go there.

A lone truck was stopped alongside the side of the road, hood open and obviously out of commission. The driver had constructed a small camp alongside the truck, complete with campfire and lean-to, as pygmies do when they make a kill too big to move. Ming was reminded of how poor and hungry this province was compared to his own. "It's a bad place to break down," Ming said, his voice more amused than sympathetic. "The driver doesn't dare leave his truck, otherwise the peasants here will tear it apart, taking the engine and other parts to sell as scrap."

An hour passed. Aside from the broken-down truck, we had not seen a single other vehicle. According to my map, this was the only land route from the southern provinces of Kwangtung and Kwangsi into the central China province of Hunan. I found it hard to believe that such an important roadway should be so lightly trafficked. Was it possible, I asked Ming, that we had taken a wrong turn? Ming shook his head, smiling over my perplexity. "This is the way traffic is all over China outside of the main cities. Kwangtung is a special case. Hong Kong Chinese have donated thousands of cars, vans, and trucks to villages and communes there. Wuchow prefecture probably has fewer vehicles than my home county in the Delta." As always, a look of unconscious satisfaction accompanied mention of the Delta.

Ming came close to being the perfect traveling companion. Most of the time he was a silent but friendly presence, never boring you with non sequiturs about the weather, places, or people. His comments were few, acerbic, and invariably instructive. With him it was possible to be by yourself, and yet not be lonely; to have company, yet not be distracted. In this he was typically Chinese, a member of a people given more to calm reflectiveness and less to wild exuberances than Americans. He was partial to his home village, county, and province, in that order, in a way that more peripatetic Americans are not, our local loyalties having been diluted by generations of constant migration, and in this also he was very Chinese.

Settlements were scattered less closely in this cleft land, and the road rarely brought us near to them. But at a place where the road curved abruptly back on itself, I espied a village far below, embraced in the bend of a bubbling stream. It was a little corner of the world that seemed deliberately tucked away from the rest, for the road half encircled the village, only to bypass it, and the river ran as if it were a moat, unbroken by any bridge or crossing. Thus enclosed, the village seemed complete in itself, a magic, enchanted world of twenty or so sturdy adobe homes. We were only twenty miles away from Wuchow, but it felt as through we were far removed in space and time. Only the electricity wires stretched along the river spoke of the present century. The rest seemed as a window opened on the distant past.

The whole was a feast of color. The pale blue of the sky was home to a slowly moving cumulus cloud of brilliant white. The mountains rolled away in soft, blue-green battalions from the picket line of the river, which wound aquamarine around garden slopes. Purple-stalked stands of sugarcane, together with bright green swatches of corn, formed a checkerboard, with its center given over to a giant square of red and ochre, the village. People with nut-brown faces and black dress moved about slowly, looking like ceramic figurines of peasants. The setting was beautific, an image of ineffable peace. Here was a place to live out the homely parabola of existence—birth, courtship, childbirth, childrearing, old age, death: the comforting compass of a small village. It was easy to be charmed by this blue-green solitude in eastern Kwangsi.

I was tempted to start down, but I could see that it would be quite a climb down to the river, and there was no boat or bridge in sight to cross. What appeared as a masterpiece of form, composition, and color from where I was standing would undoubtedly take on a quite different aspect as I approached. These practical considerations brought me back to the world of the real, in which this was just a village like any other, little different from the ones I had passed up the road.

Yet for a moment the village had appeared to be possessed of a perfect serenity—a quality that, even as I knew it was illusory, still intrigued me. I had been distracted by an idea, the notion of the romantic idyll. Dreams of an escape to a life of rustic, communal simplicity are an important part of the fantasy life of contemporary Westerners. Rousseau, living in a peasant Europe, ennobled savages, glossing over the Hobbesian realities of tribal life. Western man, living in the pressure cooker of the electronic age, romanticizes peasant life from afar, forgetting or ignoring the fact that man in nature is often pinched by poverty, racked by labor, and weakened by disease. The passing of an age makes it hard to keep it in perspective.

Of course my momentary lapse into ethnocentric fancy was mistaken in another way as well. The apparent isolation of the village was a deception, a trick of topography. Units of the Red Army had visited this area in the last days of the civil war, perhaps recruiting peasants from this very village into a struggle that they only dimly understood. Young cadres had come here in the early 1950s to flog the rich and collectivize the poor. Red Guards had been through here in the late sixties to destroy the statues of gods and the tablets of ancestors. This hamlet was a production team, part of a production brigade that in turn was part of a commune, for the production of maize and sugarcane here follows a central plan. However pristine and isolated this settlement seemed, it was nevertheless at the collared end of a long leash of power held by Peking.

Ming's reaction to my thoughts was to tell me a story about an isolated village in the rugged northeastern part of Kwangtung province that some Red Guard friends of his had stumbled across on a cross-country hike. The tiny community of six families living there had been surprised to see visitors, for they had had none in many years, but had welcomed and feasted their young guests warmly all the same. They were not part of any team, brigade, or commune, although one or two of the men did occasionally visit a village many miles away to barter for essentials like salt. For the rest, they were self-sufficient, planting corn and sweet potatoes on the mountainsides for staples, raising pigs and chickens for the occasional feast days, totally cut off from the rest of the world. "Who sits now upon the dragon throne?" the village elder had asked the startled Maoist youth.

I was fascinated by Ming's story, especially since I had heard like tales while doing research in the Delta.[2] All more or less similar, the stories seemed to be updated versions of the ancient Tale of the Source of Peach Blossoms, in which a wandering fisherman discovers a lost village living off the edge of time, where the people preserve the dress and customs of another age. This story, written in the fourth century A.D. by T'ao Yuan-ming, has long been the Chinese version of the pastoral ideal, of a simple, happy world away from the complexity and corrup-

---

[2] Simon Leys, in his *Broken Images: Essays on Chinese Culture and Politics* (London: Allison & Busby, 1979), recounts a similar tale of a tiny, lost hamlet come upon by his Chinese friend T: "T still remembers how amazed he was not to find any portrait of Chairman Mao on any of their walls" (p. 111).

tion of bureaucratic civilization. But whether Ming's tale finds its origin in truth or myth, he and the other peasants who repeated it to me were making a revealing statement about the overarching state and its incessant intrusions into their lives. A desire to escape the reach of the state and slip back into the simple, family-centered life of times past might not be surprising among the very old, hungry for the ways of their youth, but it was not from the very old that I heard these tales. It was from the young—those who, like Ming, had grown up under the new system.

The heat of midday was now upon us, and when the road descended into a tiny green valley blessed with a clear stream, we stopped. I splashed some of the water on my face and arms and found it deliciously cold, still carrying a mountain chill after its precipitous descent from surrounding peaks. The more I splashed the wetter I got, until I said to hell with it, threw my shirt on the bank, and waded in. The water was not more than three feet deep, but I let my body float on the surface, trailing my feet in the sand to hold my place in the swift flow, and lazily contemplated the bowl of the sky. It was a relief to be momentarily free of the van, the dust that roiled up from its wheels, the moist heat that crowded in its windows, and its incessant jolting.

I arrived back at the van to find it surrounded by the inevitable group of amiable villagers, puffing contentedly on the cigarettes Ming had handed out. My appearance caused them first to start and then to stare, but from these simple country folk this was not an affront. They took me in abashedly, out of the corners of sunwhipped eyes. But when I spoke with them they answered well, displaying the self-composure and slow, measured delivery natural to peasant men, who put great stock in the spoken word. I found out that we were in People Peace Commune, and that in this commune it was the team, with from ten to twenty families, that was the functioning collective. One man used a peculiarly peasant metaphor to explain: "The team is like the father. The brigade and the commune are like the ancestors, the grandfather and great-grandfather, powerful but far away."

Despite these "family" ties, the commune was riven by sharp differences in income. Although they all did the same kinds of field work, laborers in the poor hill teams earned only twenty fen a day, while those from teams that farmed the valley floor earned four times as much. Such is the difference between wet-rice agriculture and dry-land crops such as

maize or sweet potatoes. The lay of the land is everything in South
China, where even slight differences in elevation can ensure an ade-
quate supply of water in one field while baking its neighbor in the sun.
Communes were established in 1958 in part to level such differences, so
that at least within their boundaries the socialist principle of "to each according to his work" would become a reality. But as newly appointed officials proved themselves inept managers, and peasants adopted a policy
of passive resistance, it was not socialist equality, but famine, that ensued in 1959–1960. The land was returned to the villages a year later,
and the earlier inequalities reasserted themselves.

The road climbed up out of the valley toward the rugged and forbid-
ding mountains where, the peasants told us, the commune of Ancient
Dragon was situated. It certainly looked like the kind of country in
which dragons would have their lairs. But if there were such creatures,
then they would have been well advised to migrate elsewhere, for we
found that the Chinese had declared war upon these slopes. Whole
mountainsides—slopes as steep as forty-five degrees—were being gut-
ted of all life by hundreds of peasant laborers, an onslaught that left
nothing behind it but a thin layer of red, broken soil, so bright in color
that the earth itself seemed to be bleeding. A short piece down the road
we came upon another regiment of peasants, planting foot-high pine
trees and sweet potatoes in staggered rows across a series of recently
cleared mountainsides. I decided that the commune of Ancient Dragon,
probably desperate to raise agricultural production, was responsible for
this devastation.

All at once a truck with the logo of the Ministry of Forestry came
barreling around the curve ahead, stopped directly in front of us, and
disgorged a blue-suited official. He stroke to a vantage point that offered
a view of the whole. There he stood immobile, hands clasped behind his
back, a sturdy figure with head held high, eyes sweeping across the work
in progress. Like a general reviewing troops, I decided at first, but then
corrected myself: like Chairman Mao standing on a mountaintop during the Long March, urging his troops onward. This was one of the most
famous paintings of the late Chairman, not least because literally
millions of posters of the scene had been printed up during the Cultural
Revolution to bolster Mao's flagging image as the Great Helmsman.
The appearance of the official before me couldn't match the inflated

musculature and ruddy colors that Socialist Realism had given to the late Chairman, but he had the forceful posture down pat.

He proved approachable, though because he didn't relax his posture our conversation seemed to lack a certain naturalness. He assured me that what we were seeing was not, as I had assumed, a local effort. These hillsides were part of a "national forest." He, a graduate of the Peking Institute of Forestry, was in charge of this project.

It was time for some tough questions.

"Mightn't you want to leave some underbrush instead of completely denuding the hillside?"

"Want to get the entire preserve in pine trees as soon as possible."

"What about the problem of erosion?"

"That's why we plant the sweet potatoes. Their roots help to hold the soil in place for the slow-growing pine. Besides, we use the sweet potatoes to feed the camp laborers, who don't receive government rations. They are only temporary workers, peasants recruited from People Peace and Ancient Dragon communes."

The sweet potatoes may feed the workers, but they didn't anchor the soil in place very well. The gullies that creased the newly cleared slopes proved that. I must have looked dubious, because the official abandoned his heroic pose and began to talk. Slowly at first but then with the words rushing out of him like a torrent, he told me a sad tale of bureaucratic blundering and ecological mismanagement. The story began in 1958, during the Great Leap Forward, when the entire area, a chunk of land roughly seven miles wide and thirty miles long, had been designated a national forest. This did not mean, as it would have in the United States, that the area was to be reserved for recreational use but rather that it was to be managed as a huge tree farm. The newly appointed director was assigned a quota of lumber to provide to the state each year and given several hundred workers and a handful of forestry specialists to accomplish this task. My informant, newly graduated from college, had been one of the latter. From the beginning, however, things had not gone well. The distant bureaucrats who had set the quota were apparently unaware that in this part of Kwangsi, precious little forest cover had survived centuries of Chinese settlement. The director, a military man with little education and even less understanding of scientific forestry, had repeatedly failed to provide the amounts of lumber annually requisitioned by the state, even though these grew smaller over the years. Indeed, after the first couple of years, when the few remaining stands of pristine forest had been savagely felled, he had in most years not produced enough timber to cover overhead. He had planted trees that were slow-growing and had cut them down before they reached marketable size. This drain on the national budget had not been a matter of great concern under Mao, when ideological purity was more important than the bottom line. But with the coming of Teng's economic reforms, the director had been ordered to begin turning a profit. It was at this crisis that he—still the same man—had dreamed up the radical scheme of completely clearing slopes that were really too steep to tree-farm. Few of the stunted trees that were cut down provided much in the way of lumber, but along with the brush they could be sold as kindling to the lowlands and thus generate a little income.

As he talked, the forester had become ever more indignant. All at once he checked himself, perhaps fearing that he had said too much to this passing stranger, and stood silently contemplating the scene of impending desolation that stretched out before us. But he had said enough for me to finish his thoughts. The rape of these slopes is typical of inept bureaucrats, stupid and short-sighted. This red laterite soil is poor in nutrients. What soil doesn't wind up in the valleys below, reducing the fertility of the topsoil it covers, is going to be baked by the tropical sun as hard as the adobe bricks with which the peasants construct their homes. The scene is set for an ecological disaster, for in a few years these mountains are going to be badlands.[3]

Ancient Dragon turned out to be a hardscrabble place—not surprisingly, since peasants from there agreed to work for little more than sweet potatoes. But I did come upon a handful of villages there, planted securely about the rim of an almost perfectly circular valley perhaps two miles in diameter, that were better off than most. Considerably better off. The flat land was in rice paddy, and the elevations were home to

[3] The ecological consequences of the Chinese bureaucracy's efforts to exploit Chinas's resources have not been limited to deforestation. According to the specialist Vaclav Smil, China lost "an incredible 30 percent . . . of its 1957 farmland" between 1957 and 1977. Short-sighted efforts to increase grain production by means of centrally directed experiments in land reclamation, irrigation, and double- and triple-cropping have proved disastrous. See Vaclav Smil, *The Bad Earth: Environmental Degradation in China* (New York: M. E. Sharpe, Inc., 1984).

omega-shaped graves, the largest and finest I had seen since leaving Kwangtung. For leaving their descendants this rice bowl, the ancestors of this valley have been elevated to near sainthood.

We spent the next hour twisting over the hill-and-valley landscape of South China. I felt as though we were driving on a Möbius strip, that we were continually coming back to the same beginning as we rolled by village after village in valley after valley. If America is defined by her Great Plains, her vast open expanses of land, then China is defined by her snug little river valleys and basins, each of which has its covey of villages. And even here, in the Chinese midlands, there was not a level patch of ground but that it was under cultivation. What makes America what it is, said Gertrude Stein, is that: "In the United States there is more space where nobody is than where anybody is." What makes China what it is, is that there is almost no space where nobody is. There is somebody, most oftan a surfiet of somebodies, everywhere.

It is ultimately not the land but the people who demand attention, who provide a sense of place and perspective. Chinese landscape paintings were not complete until man or one of his artifacts—a bridge, a boat, or a temple—had been drawn in the foreground, as if symbolizing the constant efforts to tame, cultivate, and control nature. More than in the West, it was man, and not God or Nature, who in his ubiquity is the measure of all things in China.

The next curve brought us to the Meng Chiang, the "Concealed River," where we turned north, as always, heading upriver. Villages alternated from side to side of the river, now one on the near bank, now one on the far, for the river meandered along in great muddy loops, and the inside curve of each offered its own fertile acres of flood plain to farm.

School let out as we were passing one of the villages on the near bank, and we pulled over to watch the children march by twos out to the road. When they caught sight of the van, however, they broke ranks, the girls taking flight for the safety of nearby bushes and trees, the boys crowding up to the van with the cockiness of their age and sex. They all had on traditional Chinese peasant dress, the baggy black pajamas that were popularly known as the "T'ang style." Whether this is what the common people of the T'ang dynasty (618–907 A.D.) actually wore I didn't know, but in the Delta only very old men still clung to this mode of dress. The rest of the population had worn Western clothes. It seemed incongruous to see the ruddy, smiling faces of small boys atop the dark and dour dress of ancients, as if the two elements had been cut and pasted together. With a queue and a skullcap they could have passed for young boys of a century ago. But the Republican revolution of 1911 had spelled the end of queues. The boys all had their hair cropped short, and not a few had their heads shaved to a glistening baldness that would have done a Buddhist monk proud. "Most parents are unwilling to spend the five to ten fen a haircut costs," Ming told me as we drove on. "They prefer to have their sons' heads shaved. That way they can go for many months without a haircut. It's a way of saving money."

I was reminded of my own visit to the village barber, when the ten-fen fee turned out to include considerably more than either I or he had bargained for. The haircut began mundanely enough, with the barber cutting my hair with an ordinary pair of scissors (ordinary except that they were of German make, dated 1882, and inherited from his great-great-grandfather, who had been the village barber in his day). The barber did exclaim once or twice over the fineness and quantity of my hair, and several members of the crowd that had materialized for this occasion picked up fallen locks and clucked over their strangeness, but I was used to this sort of scrutiny and took it smiling. He then draped my face in a hot towel and began honing an ancient straight razor (also a family heirloom but not dated) on a leather strop cracked and blackened with age. I had not realized that a shave was included, and settled back in the chair (circa 1920) to enjoy it. This reaction proved premature. With the first burning scrape down the side of my face, I discovered that the family tonsorial tradition did not include the use of shaving cream. Most village men had so little facial hair that it could easily be removed dry with a few flicks of the razor. My beard is heavy. I think the barber and I both realized at the same time that he was in over his head, but considerations of face (his, not mine) kept me quiet while he slowly pulled, nicked, and scraped my chin and cheeks raw, going over some troublesome spots four or five times in painful succession.

After he realized that I was not going to complain, though, his pace picked up. The professional challenge of barbering the first "hairy barbarian" ever to sit in the family chair seemed to spur him on to ever greater exertions. He finished the last of my beard stubble with a flourish. He shaved my nose. He squared off my eyebrows. He went over my forehead, He evened out my hairline. He worked down the nape of my neck toward my shoulder blades. All the while he played to the crowd. "So much hair!" he would report each time he stopped to wipe off the edge of his razor. "Foreigners are certainly different from Chinese!" he would say as he stropped his razor for his next attack. Except for my scalp and my eyebrows, he disposed of all the hair on my neck, shoulders, and head. And the "ordering of the hair" (haircut) was not yet finished. He took a tiny silver spoon (another heirloom), its head no larger than a small safety pin, and with it began to clean out my ears. This was the occasion for another loud lesson in comparative anthropology, for it turned out that while Chinese earwax was dry and could be scraped out in small flakes, that of foreigners was moist, slightly noisome, and clung to the ear spoon in a disgusting manner. He proposed to investigate the mysteries of my nose with yet another instrument, but I waved him gently away, to his and the crowd's evident disapointment. Then, without warning, he began to chop at my neck, knead and pummel my shoulders, and vigorously swing and twist my arms, a process that he continued for some ten minutes. On later visits we came to an understanding. Eliminating the intermediate steps, we went immediately from the actual haircut to its traditional finale, a Chinese massage.

A few miles later on, I came across my first accident of the trip. The driver of an "East is Red" tractor had swerved to avoid an oncoming truck and had lost control, ramming the sheer rock face that the road skirted. The nose of the tractor was flattened and its front wheels bent clumsily underneath it, as if it were kneeling. The tractor driver squatted quietly in the shade of his crippled machine, knuckles caked with blood, his forehead discolored by a large bruise, his face pale under its dark peasant pigments. He had apparently been thrown from his vehicle at the time of collision. The truck was parked a little up the road, where its driver too was squatting motionlessly, though he looked none the worse for wear. There was the usual crowd of Chinese from neighboring villages, phlegmatic and nondescript. They drifted around the wrecked tractor, chattering in a subdued way, not stopping to ask the driver if he was hurt or what had happened. They might have been visiting an art gallery for their air of reserved detachment. The driver did not stir.

The Concealed River eventually opened up into a storybook valley several miles broad and as long as I could see. Here the river was coaxed into small irrigation ditches that crisscrossed the low-lying fields. Everywhere there was rice paddy, and it seemed that Hwang Ch'un ("Village of the Hwangs") Commune commanded an area of some prosperity. I had not gotten far in my deductions when I saw a man and a woman struggling toward us, trying to move a heavy handcart loaded with rushes up the hill. The man was pulling, his wiry arms draped over the cart's wooden handles and his sinuous body angled forward almost parallel to the ground with the effort he was making. The woman—it must have been his wife—was pushing, her head down like a draft animal and her hands flat against the back of the cart. I guessed aloud that they were taking the rushes home to burn in their stove, but Ming shook his head with a grin, pointing silently to their feet. Instead of the plastic zoris that Delta Chinese wore (when not in the fields), the couple had on sandals of woven rushes, and I understood what the rushes on the cart were destined to become. They had gathered the rushes at the river and were now headed home—some less favored hamlet in the sur-rounding hills.

As was usually the case where there were swift-flowing rivers nearby, there was a small hydroelectric station in the valley, and the villages of the commune were wired for electricity. I wasn't sure how much elec-tricity these stations generated, but I knew they had produced an enor-mous amount of raw propaganda. Peking newspapers and periodicals endlessly invoke them as evidence of the rural progress that has been wrought under Party rule. I wanted to get the peasants' own opinion on this, so we stopped not far from one little station and questioned the first few who happened along: two doughty women with adzes over their shoulders; an old man whose clothes flapped loosely on his scarecrow-like body; a gangling teenager who drew in the dirt with his big toe out of embarrassment as we spoke. Ming had told me that the people of the Meng Valley were Cantonese, but the local dialect proved almost too long a reach for me, especially in the mouth of the old man, whose gut-teral utterances I could make no sense of. Still they all seemed to under-stand me well enough, and I had Ming to help me piece together their answers.

The hydroelectric station had been built by Hwangs' Village Com-mune without any assistance from the state during one of those spasmodic bursts of mass energy that accompanied the Great Leap Forward a little over two decades ago. When the switches were thrown for the first time, speeches were made and banners were unfurled, but the coming of electricity had made little difference in the daily lives of the commune residents. While before the husking and winnowing of grain had been done by animal power and hand, there was now an electric rice mill, but those in the more distant villages prefer to use the old animal-drawn querns rather than haul their grain to the commune seat and back. Most homes now have a 25-watt bulb to illuminate their living room in the evenings, but they keep their kerosene lamps handy for use in the other rooms of the house and also during the frequent power outages. Other things remained as they had been. The water used for washing still comes from wells and is drawn by hand. That used for irrigation comes from ditches and is moved by gravity into the lower fields and by leg-driven pumps into higher ones. A few families have purchased radios, but electrical appliances such as rice cookers, irons, or clocks are unknown. Electricity's biggest impact was in allowing the wiring of a loudspeaker system throughout the commune, which brought into ear-shot of every peasant a morning-to-night mixture of martial music, government directives, and exhortations to higher production. To the peasants of Hwangs' Village, having electricity meant eating the evening meal by electric light and a day-long diet of propaganda.

We came to the town of Li-p'u at dusk. Dinner, a dish of fried noodles, was heavily dosed with garlic, for the local diner failed to meet Ming's standards. Afterwards, I set out to explore the free market. "Lichee Bank" (Li-p'u) lived up to its name, for the street that the peasants were allowed to hawk on had a bewildering variety of fruits for sale, including plums, peaches, mangoes, papayas, pomelos, and of course lichees. I walkd around trying—unsuccessfully—to chat with the vendors. In Meng Shan, twenty miles up the road, the language had still been Cantonese. True, it had been an odd, elastic Cantonese that people had stretched out on the ends of their tongues, but I could still make out many of the words. Now, somewhere between the county towns of Meng Shan and Li-p'u, we had crossed an unmarked linguistic boundary, where Cantonese settlers moving up the drainage basin of the West River had been met by Hunanese moving down the Li River. Here in Li-p'u my Cantonese got me nowhere, and my Mandarin little

further. I finally had to conscript an intelligent-looking youth to trans-
late from Mandarin into the local version of Hunanese in order to purchase a few pomelos, a kind of thick-skinned Chinese grapefruit, from a
grizzled old peasant.

We were still sixty-five miles south of Kweilin, but the strange formations for which that city was famous had already begun to appear
faintly on the horizon. With their steep sides and gently rounded tops,
they resembled nothing so much as half-loaves of French bread stood up
on the ground in rows. But we had not gone far before darkness fell, putting off closer inspection until the morrow.

Ming was going on twelve hours at the wheel but, with the stubborn
pride of the professional, would not admit that he was in the least tired,
and refused to let me spell him. He gave up the wheel only after I told
him that I really enjoyed driving, particularly at night. Never did I come
to more quickly regret a white lie.

The road was flat, straight, and, since Meng Shan, paved. I was
rolling along at perhaps fifty miles an hour when I encountered my first
truck. Like most Chinese trucks it was a copy of a 2½ ton World War II
Soviet army truck. This model's most eyecatching feature is a cattle-
sweeper-like bumper that sits about chest-high to the van driver, who
has no doubt that in the event of a collision the bumper would come right
through the front of his vehicle. I had often come upon such trucks during the day, bombing down the centers of narrow roads, scattering other
vehicles like chickens on a country lane. But I had never before encountered one at night. Remembering the tractor accident, which had
made an impression on me no amount of statistics could match, I was
keeping well to the right. We had closed to a distance of about a hundred
yards when the truck's headlights suddenly went out. Instinctively, I
hit the brakes. The incoming vehicle, lit up in the glare of my headlights, had slowed to a crawl. So had I, and in this fashion we inched
toward each other. Only when we were alongside did the truck's headlights come back on, after which it roared away, leaving the metallic
smell of diesel exhaust in the night air.

As I slowly brought the van up to speed, Ming told me that from now
on, when I encountered another vehicle at night, I was to turn off my
lights. There is a traffic regulation that only parking lights can be used at
night in places where there are oncoming vehicles. This regulation is

Day One
The never-ending search for fuel: a man collecting coal spillage.

The bounty of paddy: a whitewashed adobe home in Lupu Commune, Kwangtung.

The Vendor: taken out of school to sell peanuts at the crossing.

Day Two

The absence of paddy: The adobe homes that rise in the sugarcane groves near Te-ch'ing are plain structures. Note the quern—stone hand mill—in the foreground.

Regulating the river trade: a floating pier at Wuchow.

Along the "Concealed" River: As the river meanders, villages switch from bank to bank taking advantage of the flood plains on the river bends.

A boy of the Hakka, the "guest families" who formed the last wave of Chinese immigration into Kwangsi.

Day Three

Vegetables for the city: These peasant homes sit among garden plots of climbing squash and stringbeans, which are sold to urban residents for needed cash.

The class struggle continues: housing for commoners (foreground) and elites (background).

Cormorant fishing on the Li River near Kweilin. With increasingly serious water pollution, fishing with cormorants is becoming a rare sight in China.

Day Four

Back bent to an ancient water scoop, an old man waters his fields. Irrigation pumps are still uncommon in China.

Those who constructed this simple mausoleum may have been poor, but they were not unfilial. They chose a perfect resting place for their ancestor, one that commands the valley below.

To save the barber's fee, the parents of this boy keep him shaved.

A cowshed in a hill village. During the Cultural Revolution many people were forced to take up residence in such stalls as punishment.

strictly enforced in the cities, but not in the countryside. There drivers customarily flash their headlights every ten yards or so on an approach just to be on the safe side.

Even Ming, whom I could usually count on to criticize those features of Chinese life that were unreasonable, was convinced that this lights-out policy was putting safety first. "Look at it this way," he said. "If both vehicles have their lights on, the drivers can easily be blinded by the lights of the approaching cars." I countered, still not convinced, by pointing out that only an idiot would stare directly at the oncoming pair of lights, and that the proper thing to do was dim your lights and keep your vision fixed on the right-hand shoulder of the road. He seemed mildly nonplussed when I showed him how to dim the lights. It turned out that the headlights of Chinese trucks and headlights come without a dimmer switch.

After a second and then a third truck came barreling down out of the darkness—this was a heavily traveled road—I did come to see that turning off one's lights had at least one thing to recommend it. Drivers hit their brakes automatically when they flicked off their lights, slowing to a crawl. At five m.p.h. even a head-on collision is not going to do much damage.

As the evening wore on, and the trucks kept coming, I even began to be amused by these nocturnal encounters. Lights flicked off at 100 yards, the road a faint ribbon in the moonlight, two lumbering shapes on a collision course. They approach each other slowly, cautiously, like great, armored beasts in a sort of weird mating dance, lights flickering on and off like fireflies in silent communication. Finally they are flank to flank for a tense moment. Then, the passing consummated, they suddenly break clear, roaring off in opposite directions. Before reaching Kweilin that night I must have participated in this frantic passing play a dozen times.

CHAPTER THREE

Karst Castles

I awoke to find the mountains I had seen silhouetted against the sky the previous night now jutting up in all directions. Perhaps they were not true mountains because they were only a few hundred feet high, but they thrust themselves up out of the earth so vertically, like fins or shards, that they seemed to demand the title. These were karst formations, formed as water percolating through soft limestone leached out caves and sinkholes, eroding away the landscape until these pillars of denser limestone stood alone. Geology says that they are the hard remnants of a higher earth; instinct has it the opposite: They look as if they sprang up out of the soil like giant stalagmites.

There was something otherworldly about these formations, towering like lofty greyish-white islands over the low structures of Kweilin. Even inside the congested city, which occupied a narrow valley alongside the Li River, a few of these outlandish pinnacles had sprouted, their sheer walls crevassed and crumbling, their surface speckled with dark vegetation. In the northern district reared pyramidal Fupo Hill, where a tiger spirit was said to lurk, and beyond it Tiehtsai Mountain, the legendary home of two beautiful fox-fairy women. Overlooking the center of the city was Solitary Beauty Peak, a leaning, tapering column that seemed to defy gravity and was made more fantastic still by the small pavillion that graced its summit. Marking the city's southern border was Elephant Trunk Hill, a great hulking monolith through one end of which the river had cut a natural archway—the elephant's trunk.

The name Kweilin means "Cinnamon Forest": The Chinese annals tell us that in prehistoric days a huge forest of cinnamon trees stretched over much of northeastern Kwangsi. The city itself lies astride the easiest of all routes leading from central China to the south, and has been continuously occupied since the first emperor of the Ch'in dynasty (221–206 B.C.) undertook his campaign against the state of Nan-yueh (Vietnam). Because of its key strategic location, it was a provincial capital during the Ming and Ch'ing dynasties and again from 1936 to 1949. During these years it was an important center of resistance to the 1938 Japanese invasion of China, especially after rail links to central China and to the south were completed the following year.

But for most of its history Kweilin seems to have given itself over to pursuits far removed from politics or war. In preliberation times it was known as a city of intellectuals and artists. For a city of just under 200,000—small by Chinese standards—it has a surprising number of ancient monasteries and modern schools; already by the early decades of this century it boasted a university, a medical college, a normal college, and a technical institute. The city has also been a mecca for poets and painters (in China often one and the same), large numbers of whom have over the centuries come to this fairy landscape to try and capture its haunting beauty. The sum total of their efforts was not merely to make Kweilin famous; it was to make it into a Type. Just as the prototypical wall in the Chinese mind is the Great Wall, the very idea of a landscape is a place where fantastic pinnacles rise abruptly from lake-studded plains to break through wreaths of mist and reveal distant glimpses of ravines and waterfalls. In short, Kweilin.

In the decades before 1949, as travel in the interior of China became less arduous, Kweilin also began to draw large numbers of less exalted visitors: ordinary Chinese and foreign tourists. The Banyan Lake Hotel where Ming and I stayed was a relic from this prerevolutionary age. There was a languid antebellum air about this place. Huge overhead fans spun lazily in the high-ceilinged dining room, and ancient spotted carp floated motionlessly in a moss-covered rock pond in the courtyard.

The rooms were comfortably spare, with unvarnished wooden floors and old-fashioned beds with tubular metal frames. I calculated that the hotel had been built in the thirties to accommodate Westernized Chinese from Hong Kong. The giveaway was the bathroom, which was more than half taken up by a great enamel bathtub with giant clawed feet of the kind that was popular in the United States fifty years ago. The effect was rather like that of an inverted turtle.

The city was just beginning to receive its first sizeable influx of tourists in over forty years when I arrived, and there were indications that the local Party bureaucracy was less than comfortable with its new role. At least that's the impression I got from a fold-out tourist brochure that I picked up at the hotel's front desk. It was as good a quality of paper and printing as I'd seen in provincial China, where paper is in short supply and printing technology is limited to what the Nationalists left behind. But the beauty of Kweilin's scenic spots was not shown to best effect by the slightly blurry pictures, and the accompanying text seemed designed to deliberately discourage visitors.

"Before liberation [I read] Kweilin was a consumer city. Now it has been turned into a socialist industrial city of some scale."

The claim that Kweilin had been transformed from "a consumer city" to "a socialist industrial city of some scale" was enough to make any tourist stiffen in apprehension, if not cross Kweilin off his itinerary entirely. What tourist wants to be treated to the sight of smokestacks. Perhaps the local Communist Party bureaucracy did not know this. In the Marxist terminology they were schooled in, "consumption" had the connotation of a ravaging social disease, while "production" was next to godliness. Before the Chinese civil war, perhaps nine-tenths of the industrial might of China had been located in just two cities, Shanghai and Tientsin. Worried about the concentration of industry and the loyalty of workers in these two coastal cities relatively near Taiwan, Peking decided to site new factories inland. The central planners went to work and came up with a blueprint that would not only accomplish this decentralization, but would also remake all inland cities from centers of "consumption" to centers of "production." The plan was simple to the point of mindlessness: Factories were to be assigned to cities according to their administrative level. Each provincial capital was to have, for example, its own truck factory; each county town like Te-ch'ing was to have its own carbonated beverages facility and its own canning company; and each prefectural city like Wuchow or Chao-ch'ing was to have its own steel smelter, chemical plant, paper mill, and tractor factory. This senseless duplication was extended even to Kweilin, a prefectural capital whose extraordinary "scenic spots and relics" could easily be harmed by the pollutants produced by industry. This possibility apparently did not faze Kweilin's bureaucrats, who remain so proud of their new status as a "socialist industrial city" that they can't help bragging about it to puzzled tourists.

I read further.

"Before liberation [Kweilin's] scenic spots and relics suffered serious damage time and again. While promoting a speedy development of socialist economy, the party and the People's Government have taken effective measures to restore and protect [Kweilin's] many attractions and relics, thus making the Kweilin landscape more lovely than ever."

It didn't seem quite fair to allude to the destruction that had been visited on Kweilin in earlier times, such as when the Japanese took the city in 1944, without at the same time acknowledging the ravages of the Red Guards, who demolished many of the ancient monasteries and temples in the area in the late 1960s with Mao's encouragement.

But to me the brochure's most startling omission was the lack of any direct reference to tourism, although this activity is Kweilin's most important "industry" bar none. Since the late seventies Kweilin has become a popular resort city for Hong Kong Chinese, just as it was before the Second World War for wealthy Chinese from other cities of China. It is to cater to this trade that no effort has been spared to repair the ravages of time and the Red Guards and to make the "Kweilin landscape more lovely than ever." Yet tourism is not mentioned directly, probably because it is a purely consumer-oriented enterprise producing nothing except joy in the heart of the traveler. To the orthodox Marxists who run Kweilin, tourism is an embarrassment and its proceeds ill-gotten gains indeed.

With its masses of foreign visitors, not to mention its erudite and cultured past, Kweilin should be a cosmopolitan city, yet its inhabitants are affected by the same provincialism that I found in the other towns and cities I passed through. This comes through in small ways. While I was having dinner that night in the Banyan Lake Hotel's restaurant, two waitresses timidly approached me. Of the same slender height and pale complexion, wearing identical uniforms, plain white cotton shirts and baggy black trousers, they could have been sisters. Only their hairstyles—one wore pigtails and the other had curls—distinguished them. They had seen me writing in my notebook and had come to exclaim over the fact that I was accomplishing this task with my left hand. All Chinese are right-handed.

"Is your right hand crippled?" Pigtails asked solicitously, thinking that only a birth defect or an accident could drive a person to the extreme of left-handedness. I lifted up my right hand, which had been in my lap, and wiggled it around to demonstrate that it was a perfectly sound hand with normal dexterity.

They looked puzzled, but then Curls brightened with assurance and bubbled: "Then you can write with both hands!"

I assured them that I could not, and attempted to prove it by writing "my name is Steve" with my right hand. The awkward scrawl that emerged only proved to them that I was ambidextrous. It also created another conundrum.

"Why are some characters ["words"] long and others short? Pigtails wanted to know.

English is unlike Chinese, which consists of little square ideographs each precisely the same size, in that words vary in length. I couldn't help thinking than any youth who grew up in a city of 200,000 people and who currently works in a hotel that caters to foreign guests should know this peculiarity of alphabetical languages, which, China aside, are in use everywhere on the globe. I was unsure of where to make a start at answering her question, so I asked both of them how far they'd gone in school.

"We are upper-middle-school graduates," Curls answered. Apparently feeling that this was not a completely accurate summary, she added: "But we went to school during the Cultural Revolution, so we didn't learn very much."

"We didn't study English," Pigtails added.

After I unraveled for them the mysteries of the alphabet, I told them about my trip. They became very quiet as I described how I had come overland from Canton, about three hundred miles as the crow flies, and how I would be continuing on to Szechwan, three times that distance away. They had never been away from Kweilin, they told me. They left unstated the obvious corollary, that having been registered here at birth, having been educated in local schools, and having been assigned to work here, it is unlikely that they ever will leave.

Our conversation ended at that point because the restaurant manager came out and shooed them back into the kitchen. Since business had been slow that night, I guessed that he was worried about his waitresses fraternizing with the foreign guest.

Local Chinese and foreigners, even tourists from Hong Kong, are kept apart whenever possible. This practice had caused a discordant moment when we arrived at the Banyan Lake Hotel. The manager had at first refused to allow Ming to register, saying that the hotel was limited to foreigners and Chinese living abroad. I argued that it was too late in the day for Ming to find other accommodations, but he remained adamant. The state directive concerning acceptable clientele, he said, specifically excluded local Chinese. Only after I told him that I would leave unless Ming was permitted to stay did he cave in. Later, after Ming and I had observed that the hotel was empty except for a dozen Hong Kong tourists, we laughed that he was probably under pressure to improve his occupancy rate. The pressure of the market is invariably democratic.

I had forgotten that unpleasant episode of apartheid by the following morning when we set out to see the city's most famous set of limestone caves, the Ch'i Hsing Yen or Seven Star Cave. A long line stretched out in front of the ticket office, where a sign read "Tickets: 20 fen." Ming urged me to go to the head of the line, saying with his secret smile that it was expected of a foreigner, but I preferred to stand in line like the others. The line soon grew longer with the addition of a group of young workers from a local Kweilin chemical factory. We chatted away, all happy to be temporarily freed from our respective routines—I from the rigors of the road, they from the rather nauseating confines of their factory. When I reached the ticket office I handed the ticket seller, a young woman with short bangs, forty fen for two tickets. It turned out not to be enough. "For foreigners it's forty fen a ticket," the woman said in a fishwife's voice. It was an expensive admission price for China, where theater tickets are only ten or twenty fen, and I heard the figure repeated in startled whispers by the young workers I had been talking with. I felt as though I were being fined for the color of my hair. The only difference between my tour and theirs was the tickets themselves: My forty-fen ticket was larger than the twenty-fen tickets of my factory acquaintances and was printed in color instead of black on white. Ming couldn't resist putting in his oar. "The authorities intend for you to keep it as a souvenir," he offered slyly of the ticket.

The Kweilin workers and I nevertheless walked together, as members of the same tour group, through Fish Dragon Gate into the first of the seven interconnecting caverns that comprised the cave. The limestone interior had been sculptured by running water into a gallery of Chinese folk tales. We were shown the Prince's Platform, the Clouds of Heaven, the Two Dragons Fighting for a Pearl, the Monkey Stealing Fairy Peaches, and Three Stars After a Snail, along with a menagerie of lions, tigers, camels, frogs, and fish. My Kweilin friends whispered that there was said to be a legend to accompany each of these formations, though they added that they themselves were too young to know them. If our tour guide knew, she wasn't saying. The only tale we heard from her concerned the Bottomless Pit, before which she said shortly: "In preliberation times the superstitious used to throw live fish into this pit to accumulate virtue for the next life. Since the Liberation, such feudal customs are no longer practiced." She may have been right. Even though I stood as close to the opening of the pit as I could, I caught no whiff of rotting fish.

Pricewise, the experience of the cave reminded me of my first trip to China, when I had paid three times what the locals paid for the same second-class coach ticket from the Hong Kong border town of Shenchun to Canton. It had been my first lesson in one of the basic facts of life in the Middle Kingdom, that the prices of goods and services vary depending on who is doing the buying. During my stay in the village, living in my own house and buying meat and vegetables in the local peasant market, I had been mostly insulated from this double standard. Now I was encountering it again, and the unfairness of it irked me. I was paying thirty-two yuan a night for a room in the Banyan Lake Hotel that, though it had its own bath, was smaller than the room Ming and I had rented for only five yuan the night before in a Chinese hostel. At six yuan, the price of Chinese breakfast at the Banyan Lake—rice congee (again), with small dishes of roasted peanuts, shredded white fish, and pickled vegetables—had raised Ming's eyebrows. It was, he had estimated for me, about six times what the meal was worth. And when my laundry came back that evening and the bill was nearly five yuan for only two shirts and one pair of pants, we were both aghast. "At those prices, why bother to have clothes washed?" Ming had groaned. "You could buy new ones cheaper."

I had heard officials attempt to explain away the two-tiered price system by saying that many services, such as rail transportation, are state-subsidized, and that it is only fair that "rich foreigners" should not enjoy a fare break intended for "poor Chinese." But it was hard for me to imagine that tourist attractions receive much in the way of government subsidies. The overhead of the Seven Star Cave, for example, is limited to the cost of lighting the caverns for each passing group, and the one-yuan-a-day wages of the tour guides, each of whom daily escorts hundreds of ticket holders through the cave. Even if foreigners paid only twenty fen a ticket, here was a state-run enterprise that could scarcely fail to make a hefty profit.

When pressed on this point, one official admitted that prices for foreigners are set following "international norms"—that is, the cost of meals and hotel rooms in socialist China is pegged to the going rate in capitalist Taiwan and Hong Kong. No matter that the quality of the socialist food, lodging, and services provided in return often falls miserably short of capitalist "norms," as when at the Banyan I found the hot water so red with rust that I opted for a cold sponge bath instead. But it is not merely exploiting the casual tourist that is at stake here. That happens everywhere, though governments are rarely so involved in the game. The unequal treatment of foreign tourists is but one example of the predisposition of the Chinese bureaucracy (while publicly extolling classlessness) toward endlessly fragmenting society along lines of class, rank, and status. In China nothing—neither prices, nor housing, nor justice—is equal for all. And everywhere I went in Kweilin that day, I kept stumbling across the fracture lines.

When I was out of the van taking pictures of Kweilin streets, I noticed that a motorcycle with sidecar, still a frequent sight in China, had pulled up alongside Ming. I headed back to the van in time to overhear the policeman quietly ask Ming if he was "driving this foreign guest around?" Ming nodded with great gravity, upon which the policeman said loudly, with a show of politeness, that "Comrade driver" should "drive carefully," and waved us on our way.

"That was close," Ming said with real relief in his voice. "Until you reappeared, I was afraid that they were going to take me to the public security office."

I gave Ming a quizzical glance.

"They said that we had stopped in a no parking zone," Ming explained. "They wouldn't have said anything if we were driving a car, for they would have known that you were an official or a foreigner. But they saw that it was a van and thought that the passengers were only Hong Kong Chinese. You should have heard them before you returned. They were yelling at me and threatening to take me in.

"It's worse when I'm driving a truck," he continued as we drove on. "They know that truck drivers have no power or influence, and they haul you in on the slightest pretext. Truck drivers are looked down on as the lowest class of motor vehicle drivers." Then his face lightened into his habitual smile: "Of course, even truck drivers rank higher than the drivers of tractors or horse carts."

That ranking certainly held in Kweilin, where the entire city was closed to tractors and horse carts. Trucks were allowed in on the side roads, but were forbidden to use the main thoroughfares. Only half-a-dozen cars were in sight on the four-lane avenue called (what else?) Liberation Road that we were driving down. What harm could be done opening such avenues for truck traffic? Ming smiled knowingly at the rows of buildings in the new style that lined the road. "This is where the city's party committee has its offices, and where many officials live. They don't want to have the streets they live and work on overrun with noisy trucks belching black fumes. Better to keep them in the 'production areas' of cities, where the factories and workers' domitories are located."

But it was most of all an incident that occurred at Reed Flute Cave (Lu Ti Yen) later that afternoon that made painfully clear the gulf that separated Ming from me—and from the ruling class of his own country. We had arrived at the Reed Flute Cave, which was some distance outside of the city, just after the last guided tour of the day had gone in. Too late to join the tour, we had instead walked across a short causeway to a reception center on the slope opposite, which was not shown on my tourist map. The spot was well chosen, for it offered a spectacular view of the lyrically named Peach Blossom River (Tao Hwa Chiang) winding through a row of karst castles. Walking inside, I found the center filled with officials in identical blue Mao suits, looking like rows of stand-up Kewpie dolls. My appearance in their midst created a small rush of whispers, and in a second every official in the room was regarding me with the curious half-stare of their class, faces held noncommittal and expressionless. I couldn't help thinking how their behavior, seemingly devoid of human warmth, contrasted with the rough friendliness of the ordinary country people I had been meeting.

I looked around, missing Ming's friendly presence. I thought that he had followed me in, but he was nowhere to be seen. It was at that instant that I heard angry voices at the entranceway, one of which sounded like Ming's. I hurried out and found him in an argument with a uniformed young woman, that was growing more heated by the moment. "The masses aren't allowed in here," she was screaming at him. She pointed to a sign that I had not noticed on the way in. "No admission" was written on it in bold characters. "This is a reception center for officials."

"You are cheating [*ch'i-p'ian*] Chinese," Ming shouted back. He was about to say more when I grabbed his arm and pulled him away. "Leave it," I said. "There's nothing inside to see anyway."

"But you don't know what she did," he told me heatedly, still upset. "I was walking a few steps behind you. When she saw you coming, she pulled that sign out of the way. After you passed, she pulled it out again and set it down right in front of me. I tried to follow you in anyway but she stopped me. It's unfair. It's a cheat."

Ming went on grumbling for a long time before he calmed down. This explosive, anarchic anger was a side of Ming I had not seen before. He usually masked his feelings with a Mandarin composure, at most allowing himself a sarcastic remark and a secret smile or two. I wondered guiltily if I had not contributed to his outburst by my impassioned defense of equality earlier in the day. Then again, I thought, drivers are a proud, independent lot. He probably would have spoken out anyway, instead of just automatically kowtowing to authority.

Still, there was a sense in which I was responsible, for had I not entered the reception center it would never have occurred to Ming to go in. All Chinese grow up with the knowledge that their country is sharply divided into officials, workers, and peasants, in that order, and that these castes do not mix and rarely intermarry. As a peasant, Ming instinctively knew his place, and understood that he was not welcome in the pleasure gardens of the elite. However much the unfairness of the class system rankled, he would never have deliberately set out to test its limits. Nor would I, for that matter, though I was not happy over the way my friend had been publicly humiliated. The episode called to mind the shameful signs that had once hung over park entrances in that bastion of Western colonial imperialism, the Shanghai concession: "No dogs or Chinese allowed." If altered to read "No workers or peasants allowed," such signs could accurately hang over the thousands of "reception centers," "health spas," and "resorts" run by the government for China's Communist elite, similar to the one we had yesterday passed on the road. This time I spared Ming my thoughts.

I had already had enough of Kweilin's mountains, caves, and temples, feeling surfeited of dead excretions of geography and culture, but it was too late in the day to leave. The best I could do was cross back through the city and drive south along the Li River to Pagoda and Tunnel Hills, the most distant attractions shown on my map. At least Ming and I would get to see a village or two en route.

We broke suddenly from narrow, congested, working-class-neighborhood streets into the openness of the countryside. What in other countries would have been suburbs or slums was here a garden, with peasant huts standing singly about. Their style was new to me, for they were built low, and of an ancient timber that had long since weathered to a dark brown, and had latticework windows that gave them a Japanese cast. The connection was more than incidental, I realized with a start. Western China had once been covered by vast deciduous forests, and up until the late middle ages China's villages, towns, and temples had been constructed of wood. As China's population expanded over the centuries the forests had shrunk, until the Chinese had been forced back on mud and clay for their constructions in all but a few areas. But during the Tang dynasty (618–907 A.D.), before the forests had been exhausted and when Chinese culture was spreading to an awakening Japan, Chinese villages must have looked like this, just as traditional Japanese kimonos also harken back to sartorial fashions in Tang China. These huts were architectural survivals of an earlier age.

As if to say "no tourists beyond this point," the road ended at the intersection of Tunnel and Pagoda Hills. Tunnel Hill lived up to its name. Halfway up its 100-foot height gaped a hole large enough to drive the van through. Legend had it that the hole had been shot open with a bow and arrow by the Chinese general Chao T'o, who lived 2,200 years ago. Later appointed the King of Nan-Yueh (Kwangtung and Kwangsi) by the Han court, Chao T'o was the man who more than any other brought this huge area permanently inside the political and cultural sphere of the Han Chinese. Shooting a hole in solid rock with a bow and arrow seemed the perfect metaphor for his vast accomplishments in real life.

Pagoda Hill was a disappointment. The seven-story ''pagoda'' that had looked so impressive from a distance turned out to be only a small-scale replica when proximity brought it into perspective, eyeballing in at only about twelve feet high. It was like setting off to see a castle only to arrive in front of a papier-mâché model whose ridiculous ramparts reach no higher than the waist. Still, it was the first pagoda I had seen, and there was something in the purity of its lines and the nobility of its crown that was reminiscent of the majestic, centuries-old pagodas that had been the glory of old China. Had I been able to uncover any interesting local legends about it, I would have been willing to forgive its meagerness entirely. But the pagoda had no tale to tell.

What saved the scene for me were the fishermen I had spotted below on the Li River. They were using trained cormorants—avian predators that can catch fish up to $1\frac{1}{2}$ pounds in weight but are prevented from swallowing their captured prey by choker rings around their necks. This exotic way of hunting fish is still common in South China, and I was charmed by the fishermen with their feathered hooks and bamboo rafts. The lengths of bamboo had been treated by heat so that the lashed-together whole formed a pleasing curve, both ends of the craft lifting gracefully clear of the water. The cormorants perched on bow or stern, while the men stood amidships, reaching out occasionally with a length of bamboo to pole the craft to a new spot, or to prod their reluctant predator into the water to hunt. With their wings clipped to prevent them from flying away, the birds were so tame that they could be worked without a leash. I snapped off a dozen pictures almost by reflex. But as I snapped, I saw the birds go down several times and come up with their beaks empty, and the basic improbability of the scene forced itself into my consciousness. Could these middle-aged peasant men actually make a living for themselves and their families off the efforts of one or two scrawny, bedraggled birds? I stepped over to the spongy bank of the river as one of the fishermen poled his raft in.

"Good catch?" I asked in a friendly way, leaning over to peer into the large bamboo basket sitting in the middle of the raft. At first I thought it was empty but then I spotted a single glassy-eyed perch, as long as my hand, lying still in the bottom.

"Not bad," he replied.

Not bad? One fish worth perhaps fifty fen (thirty cents) for a day's work? But it came out that a good day was two or more fish, a bad day was no fish, and an average day—"not bad"—was one fish. The fisherman said he averaged only about fifty fen a day, besides what he earned from the collective's garden plot. Like many rivers and lakes in China, the Li River was polluted from factory effluents, and the fish population had declined dramatically. "Too many birds, too few fish," the man complained laconically, adding that he rarely ate fish himself. He had a state quota to meet, and was usually behind. It occurred to me as I got back in the van that between the man and his bird, the bird had the better deal. While the bird had to give up most of the fish it caught to the man, the smallest ones could still be swallowed under the choker ring. The man, chokered by the state, had to give up every last tail.

When I told this to Ming he was silent for a few moments, and then proceeded to give me a rare look into his own past. I had known about his military service, but had always assumed that he had returned immediately to the village after his discharge. It turned out that the state had made other plans. "My whole battalion was processed out of the army at once and then ordered to Wuhan [an industrial city along the middle Yangtze]. We were to be part of the labor force of a new steel factory there. I stayed for two years, but I hated it, the heat, the noise, the rationing, the crowding. I escaped back to Kwangtung. Since I had left Wuhan without permission from the authorities, I didn't have any household registration in my own village. I was a black [illegal] resident. I couldn't get any grain, nor could I work for the collective. Instead I repaired an old canal punt, replacing its rotted bottom, and started fishing on the West River. The fish I caught I bartered for rice, and in this way managed to feed my family. I was lucky because the local village head, who knew about my fishing, turned a blind eye to it. He said I wasn't registered in the village and so did not come under his authority. You see, I could have been criticized or punished for what I was doing. It was illegal. The fish in the river belong to the state. So do the fish here.''

We came back past the twin humps of Camel Hill toward the city. As we approached Liberation Bridge, formerly named Eternal Almsgiving Bridge, the sun was setting behind low and ragged clouds, bathing the Li River in pink chutes of shifting light. How magnificent Kweilin was with its many limestone bulwarks—the solitary pinnacles of the city proper, the grey-layered eminences of more distant peaks. It was a good time and place to appreciate Kweilin's extraordinary beauty.

Across the river, others were also enjoying the view and the cooling breeze that came off the river. There was a row of six-story apartment buildings, luxurious by Chinese standards, built closely overlooking the river. Each apartment had its own balcony, bringing the full sweep of Kweilin's scenery into view, and nearly all were occupied. There were also people walking along the shore beyond Fupo Hill. There a row of villas began, large one- and two-story dwellings surrounded by high walls, each with its own shaded gardens, interior courtyards, and private walkway along the river.

''City officials,'' came the terse answer to my question about who lived in the high-rises.

And further up the river behind Fupo Hill?

The municipal and prefectural party bigwigs.

Beyond this thin line of privilege along the river, old Kweilin began. Masses of narrow brick homes of uneven height and uncertain pedigree crowded together along the narrow streets like animals in a storm. They blocked any view of the natural beauty beyond, but to the residents this was of less consequence than their stultifying effect on the river breeze. The bricks burned a ruddy red in the late afternoon sunlight, and the air in the street stood still and close. But it was even hotter inside, where the women stood sweating over their woks, and the men sought the street. They sat on rickety wooden chairs or three-legged stools in their undershirts, cooling themselves with heart-shaped palm leaf fans.

In the countryside, too, there was division. The truck gardeners and cormorant fishers living in the shadow of the city were the advantaged, for the city needed their vegetables and fish and traded with them. Beyond this, out of sight but surrounding me in every direction, was the great rural sink of poverty, with its disadvantaged peasants who lived from hand to mouth. It was—that late afternoon view of city and countryside—a miniature of the rigid class structure I was immersed in, a model of Chinese society.

Still, within their carefully drawn compartments the Chinese go about their lives in much the same fashion as people everywhere. I took away one memory from Kweilin that will always give me pleasure. It is a picture of the pool in the interior courtyard of the Banyan Lake Hotel, with its moss-covered rocks and ancient carp. Evening had fallen, but the courtyard is bathed in a soft light that has escaped through the curtains of the surrounding rooms. A young man wearing the white coat of a hotel employee sits down on one of the larger rocks. The fish school by his rock like a flock of hungry park pigeons, but he sits motionless, waiting. Before long he is joined by a young woman, whose head of curls I recognize from the hotel restaurant. She sits down on the same rock, so close to her companion that their bodies are practically touching. The young man talks animatedly, while she unwraps a small package. Together the couple feed to the fish the termite eggs she has brought. As they do, they talk softly with each other. Their voices don't carry. Their warm glances, gestures, and smiles do. It is like watching a silent movie of a courtship, and I am convinced that it will be successful.

Whereas the previous evening I had felt sorry for the young woman I had nicknamed Curls for not being able to leave Kweilin, tonight I saw that she should be counted among the fortunate, and not just because she had a beau. Both she and her friend had good jobs, "iron rice bowls" guaranteed by the government, with retirement and medical benefits. On their days off they could visit the Seven Star Cave, and go on picnics beside the Peach Blossom River. If they married, they would be assigned state housing. This would be cramped, but in the (admittedly unlikely) event that either one rose high enough in the hierarchy there would be an apartment along the river, with a balcony that opened the panorama of the city up to view and caught the evening breezes. They would be allowed only one child, but it would be born in a hospital, had an excellent chance of graduating from high school, and would be awarded with an "iron rice bowl" of its own when it came of age. Kweilin may be a provincial city five hundred miles from the coast, but any city was a haven of privilege and leisure compared to the countryside. There were, I knew, far worse places in China to have to spend one's life.

Middle China

"TROUBLE ahead," Ming pointed with his chin up the road. A blue-suited public security official was standing on the shoulder of the road frantically waving a little red flag at us. He looked like a matador with a case of nerves. Ming pulled over.

"What is your destination?"

"Liuchow," Ming replied, naming the Kwangsi city that was our day's destination.

"And then?"

"Szechwan."

"Does this foreign guest have a travel permit?" he questioned Ming. I answered in the affirmative, and handed it to him. He examined it briefly and handed it back to me without comment.

"Drive carefully"—he was still speaking to Ming—"and don't stop for any hitchhikers." He made a gesture of dismissal with his flag to indicate that the interview was over.

"Don't stop for any hitchhikers?" I asked after we were back on the road.

"Must be having trouble around here with bandit gangs," Ming answered shortly.

Bandits have always formed a part of the life of Kwangsi province.

When the poet Li She was captured by bandits, he was ordered to produce an impromptu example of his art for his captors, who despite being rough men, were nevertheless Chinese. The following earned his immediate release:

> The rainy mist sweeps gently
> Over the village by the stream,
> When from the leafy forest glades
> The brigand daggers gleam . . .
>
> Yet there is no need to fear
> Or step from out their way,
> Since more than half the world
> Consists of bigger rogues than they!

It seemed doubtful if present-day Chinese bandits remained the romantic rebels of Li She's day, but it seemed well to keep the verse in mind on the odd chance than they did.

The road passed two leaning towers of limestone, the shorter of which sheltered a small village like a kind of natural lean-to. No sooner had I stepped out of the van with my camera when a chunky young villager who looked to be in his late teens came trotting over and greeted me in a friendly fashion. "This is White Sands," he volunteered, "and I am Little Horse." There was, I was instantly sure, a small stream with a bank of white sand near here, just as I would have bet that a few minutes of observation would have revealed Little Horse's equine characteristics. Rural Chinese names are for the most part reliably literal. He invited me to come to his house in the nearby village and have a cup of tea. Nothing like peasant hospitality, I thought. "I would be honored," I said, "but let me just take a picture or two first." Little Horse then walked over to the driver's side of the van and started talking rapidly to Ming. "No, we don't want any," I heard Ming say after a minute. Little Horse said something else, and Ming again declined. At that, he walked away without saying so much as a word to me, his invitation of a few moments before forgotten.

"He wanted to sell us some musk deer oil," Ming explained. "But his price wasn't right. Can you imagine, *she-hsiang* for only twenty yuan a catty! If it were real, it would sell for at least fifty yuan. Probably going to pawn off some peanut oil scented with the monkey flower on us."

The musk deer is a small, hornless, deer-like animal found in Asia. The male, besides having long canine teeth, has a gland under the skin of its abdomen that secretes musk, a very valuable substance used in expensive perfumes.

"Is it legal for him to sell it?" I was less interested in Ming's suspicions about the man's wares than in his livelihood.

"In poor areas like this, many people make a living off the mountains," Ming responded, going on to quote a folk saying: There are poor people, but no poor mountains. "There are a lot of medicinal herbs growing wild in the hills, if you know what to look for. There are also animals like moles, rabbits, and deer that can be hunted. It provides food and something to sell in the market towns. Of course, during the Cultural Revolution people were forbidden to engage in such 'capitalist'"—the word came out accompanied by his secret smile—"activities outside of the collective. If they were caught, they would be criticized and their catch or find confiscated. Even now you are supposed to sell things like medicinal herbs to the state purchase stations, but some areas are lax."

A few miles down the road I stopped to take a picture of some distant karst formations that wandered across the horizon like a topologist's doodle. I stayed to watch an old man work a water scoop (*hu-t'ou*), an irrigation device that I had read about but had never expected to see. The date of its invention was lost in time, but it had been known in the Old Kingdom of ancient Egypt, four thousand years ago, and its use in China probably dates from at least that time. As befitted its great age, it was a simple affair, a long-handled scoop slung on a rope from a bamboo tripod centered over an irrigation canal. The scoop, which was a basket lined with oilcloth, skimmed a gallon or two of water off the canal surface at the bottom of its swing, and spilled the water thus collected into the adjacent rice paddy as it reached the top of its swing. I turned my attention from the machine to its human motor. The morning coolness had already condensed into humid heat, and the old man had taken off his shirt and rolled up his baggy trousers. His chest was narrow, his legs bony, and grizzled hair framed his deeply lined face. He was, I estimated, around sixty-five years of age. Yet he worked steadily, throwing his slight body into each downward plunge of the scoop, and pumping through to raise the water up its three-feet arc into the paddy.

Again came the feeling that I'd had several times since beginning this journey, that I was traveling not just in space but in time, and had somehow driven into the seventeenth century. The only things that gave evidence of a later century, aside from my van, were the tarmac road and the electric wires that ran parallel to it. And these seemed strangely disconnected from the peasant world I was seeing. What did passing trucks mean to the youngster who spent his time combing the hills on foot for deer or herbs? And the electricity conducted by the wires did not help the elderly peasant to move water from the canal to the fields that fed him and his family.

As an Asian country breaks away from the poverty line and the standard of living begins to climb, the first to benefit are the very young and the very old. These two groups are paroled from their life sentence of hard labor, the young temporarily to attend school, the old permanently to attend to leisure. It is a measure of China's poverty that the very young and the very old must still work very hard.

One of our gas cans had started leaking, filling the van with fumes, and Ming stopped in the town of Li-p'u to look for some hard soap to calk it with. I felt that I had rejoined the twentieth century, at least the early decades. Li-p'u was the local county seat, and had a population of perhaps 40,000. Like other towns of its size, it recalled the turn of the century. Its narrow, dirty streets were perpetually lined with peasants hawking produce; its public noodle shop was furnished with high-backed wooden picnic benches and had a large ceiling fan that circled slowly overhead and did nothing to dispel the heat or the flies; and its soda parlor sold an evil sarsparilla, which quenched your thirst by killing all desire for beverages (and reminded me again that in China it was more blessed to produce than to consume). Cities of Kweilin's dimensions were usually stuck in the 1930s, at best generating the Banyan Lake Hotel's sense of prewar modernity. Scattered TV aerials poking above brick walkups and diesel buses belching black fumes gave metropolises like Canton and Shanghai a late-forties to early-fifties air. Dating the cities was easy; placing the countryside was not, because there were too few markers to work with. Villages often seemed totally outside of time.

Ming's initial effort to calk the leaking gas can left the inside of the van still reeking of gasoline, and he stopped to try again a half an hour later. The road had just breached a line of low hills, bringing the valley below into view, and I climbed the nearest hill to gain a better perspective of the whole. I was standing on the lip of a natural amphitheater, so immense that its far edge was colored with the blue-grey haze of distance. Its floor was a carpet of interlocking paddy fields of emerald green broken only by the orange-brown speckles of villages, and its sides were draped with the darker green hues—in the distance almost blue—of the hillside. Through the whole meandered a river, and by a trick of topography and distance this flow seemed totally a creation of the amphitheater, as if it were released by a hidden spring in the near hills only to be gathered up by a hidden sump in the far. I concentrated as I took in this blue-green seclusion in the hills of central Kwangsi. I wanted to hold in my mind this valley, these villages, these hills.

I was not alone on the hill. Occupying its highest point was a grave, a waist-high and man-length pile of packed earth. Several large stones had been set at the head of the grave and served as a tombstone. But there was no plaque, and I could not know who had been buried there or when. It made a poor showing compared with the elaborate headstones I had seen on older graves, but the work had still been carefully done, the stones carefully set into place without mortar, and the earth tamped into a perfect oblong shape. The grass had even been cropped back away from the grave, probably during the "bright and clear" festival held a couple of months ago in April, a day when rural Chinese visit their family graves to "sweep" them—to repair the ravages of time and weather, to present an offering of food and rice wine, and to burn incense and paper money. I was certain that if I came back the following year, or even a decade hence, the grass would not have encroached on the tomb, and its stones would still be in place. Those who constructed this simple mausoleum may have been poor, but they were not unfilial.

The ancestor was to be envied. The hill was freshened by a cool breeze, and tiny flowers grew in bouquets among the grasses. From his grave he could command the valley where he had lived out his days. It was a perfect resting place, and I left it reluctantly.

As we descended into the valley we found ourselves in the midst of frenetic activity. A hundred sandal-shod, black-jacketed men working with adzes and shovels were trenching the sides of the dirt road; a hundred others were refilling the trenches with rocks. The way was being widened, and would be paved. Except for the final step, the laying down of the asphalt, the work was being done entirely by manual labor, by hand. But those phrases do not convey the sense of the brute, animal energy being expended: men heaving up hods of dirt, quick-stepping a carrying pole load, and using slings to carry in tandem impossibly large stones.

It was Mao, with his repeated ''mobilizing of the masses,'' who had made such scenes as this famous in the West, but a reliance upon corvée labor to build roads, bridges, and river dikes is as old as China itself. One of the most famous pre-1949 examples of this took place in 1928 in this same province of Kwangsi when 152,000 people, including farmers, soldiers, and schoolchildren, were put to work building roads. By the spring of 1929, according to the provincial government, 2,000 miles of roads had been completed, and the province boasted one of the best systems of highways in China. The road now being widened by the masses may have been built by their grandfathers.

I stopped to talk to a work crew enjoying a well-deserved rest. They were peasants drafted from the local villages, and they were paid one yuan a day for their labor. It was a wage they were pleased to get, for as one solid-looking young man wearing a dirt-stained undershirt put it, ''It's more than we get in the fields.'' That amount ranged from ninety fen a day in the settlements along the river down to a bare-bones twenty fen a day for those in the surrounding hills.

It seemed a large disparity for such a narrow compass, especially after it came out that the whole—valley and surrounding hills—constituted a single commune of 18,000 people. Not that the Communist Party hasn't tried to level incomes within ''Cultivating Virtue'' (Xiuren), as the commune was called. During the Great Leap Forward, hill and valley land had been pooled—with the result that production had dropped drastically.[1] During the Cultural Revolution, rural markets were closed and sideline activities forbidden, and peasant incomes took another nose dive. Each time the Party set out to equalize wealth, it paradoxically created misery.

Under Teng, the villagers said, the income differences between

[1] The usual explanation for declining grain production during this time, poor weather, seems to have been much less important than peasant resistance and poor planning. See Nicholas Lardy, *Agriculture in China's Modern Development* (Cambridge: Cambridge University Press, 1983), p. 42.

villagers in the valley and those in the hills were increasing year by year. Valley peasants had a ready market for their surplus vegetables and handicraft products in the rural market located in the nearby commune town. The hill peasants barely grew enough on their poor fields for their own needs, besides being too far away from the market to visit it often. With these natural hill/valley inequities locked into place by rigid government regulations against geographic mobility, it is difficult to see what the hill peasants could do to raise their standards of living up to parity with those of the valley folk.

The stocky peasant had emerged as the spokesman for the group, the other members of which seemed sunk into a kind of stupor of tiredness, and he answered my questions.

On bikes: "I have a bike, but only a handful of families in my team have a bike or even a radio."

On electricity: "Each house has a light bulb, but the electricity only comes on for a few hours every evening. We use the river for water."

On birth control: "I have five children, the youngest five years of age. [This delivered with a verbal swagger.] Ah Heng here has only one. [Now a hint of condescension.] There are no rewards for having only one child, but there are fines and meetings to attend if you have a third. Happily, my youngest child was born several years ago when there were no fines."

On ancestry: "We people here came from the Hweichow area [northeast of Canton] 150 years ago. At that time only a few Chwang [an ethnic minority I was to encounter up the road] lived here and they planted only one rice crop a year. Our ancestors began planting two crops a year after they arrived. They grew in number quickly and soon drove the Chwang off."

"They drove the men off. The women they married," another man interjected, and the group guffawed.

The conversation left me puzzled and slightly dissatisfied, but we were some distance down the road before I understood why. Like most of my recent conversations with peasants, it had not been, properly speaking, a conversation at all, but a straight-line interview, an almost Pavlovian question-response. The stocky peasant had answered my questions willingly enough, and once my inquiries had even sparked debate, as several peasants permitted themselves opinions on their ancestors' settlement of the valley. But neither he nor his fellows had asked a single question.

The more I thought about this, the more the peasants of Cultivating Virtue seemed to me to have been a profoundly incurious lot. Here I was, a sandy-haired, blue-eyed Westerner, a foreign devil in the flesh. I had told them that I was from America, in Chinese the "Beautiful Country," where people were rumored to possess fabulous wealth. I had casually mentioned that I had lived in Kwangtung, the province of their ancestors, whose hoary deeds continued to be matters of debate and speculation. And none of this had stirred their imagination or piqued their interest. Squatting languidly in the shade of a roadside tree, slowly fanning themselves with their woven bamboo hats, they spoke of their families and their valley, not once lifting their thoughts past the rim of hills that girded their closed world. Perhaps they were so well adapted to their habitat that they would have felt themselves lost if they ventured outside it, even in their thoughts.

It had once been that way in the Pearl River Delta. I remember an evening around a rickety wooden table with the local village savant, a teller of tales and collector of traditional lore. He always squatted on his chair rather than sitting in it, looking a little like a roosting chicken. "We peasants like to sit this way," he would say, but this old relic of seventy was the only one I ever saw who did. Young villagers had learned to sit on chairs. What he described to me that evening, drawing out the details with great relish, were the "Eight wonders of River's End." River's End was the delta island of approximately 100 square miles that he was from. The wonders speak for themselves. There was "The Leafless Well"—an ancient open well that by some Merlinian magic kept itself perpetually free of flotsam; "The Bamboo Mist"—a local grove of bamboo which when enveloped by mist seemed to give birth to all manner of weird, diaphanous creatures; and six more creations of local fancy. But with the passage of time they were no more. Some had been destroyed, others had simply fallen into neglect. From his perch my savant sadly bemoaned the decline of these wonders, saying that only the elderly even knew of their existence. The young didn't care.

The world had expanded in size and complexity since this man's youth, and what had been contained within the old borders and lifeways had been diminished by that process. Who cared if the old well near the big oak tree had no leaves if you could get a job in a rural factory or, better yet, escape to Hong Kong? No grove of bamboo, even one said to be bewitched, is worth visiting when you can watch Hong Kong kung-fu programs on a TV set in your living room. An electronic box that can conjure up fighting ghosts simply casts a more binding spell than a grove of floating spirits.

In the mountain valley I was now in, the world still cleaved to its old dimensions. For the peasants who lived here this constituted the limits of the known world and their thoughts rarely ventured outside of it. The same self-contained landscape that coiled villages into pockets of valley still bound their thoughts: a constricting geography transformed into an ecology of the mind. I didn't ask, but it wouldn't have surprised me if there had been a well in the commune of Cultivating Virtue that leaves somehow never fell into, and that it was the object of much wonder.

The endless villages began to take on a curious similarity. As each jumbled cluster of mud-brick buildings comes into view, you look in vain for some distinguishing mark, but you find none. There is the same collective headquarters, larger but more decrepit-looking than the homes that surround it. There is the same trampled earth square where mass meetings are held on the days when state directives arrive. As always, there are women crouched beside the stream beating clothes with smooth sticks to clean them. As always, there are men squatting about, arms resting on knees, comfortably immobile in the shade of the collective headquarters. A handful of dirty boys in tattered clothes run down an alleyway past the small barefoot girl who can't run because she has her baby brother strapped on her back. A grey water buffalo stands stolidly under its little thatched pavilion, waiting to be led once more into the now empty fields. This village seems so much like the one you just left that impressions blur, and you wonder if the road isn't curving back to take you through the same decrepit hamlet again and again, with a few minor props added or taken away by the players to keep you from discovering that you are on a closed circuit. But you have never been here before. It is just that you have seen too many hundreds like it since setting out from Canton, a repetition that condenses the singularity of each village into a shared recollection of a hundred villages.

Even though you are unlikely to ever pass this way again, you do not stop. Your notebook stays closed, for there is nothing about this poor place that commends itself to your memory. The next curve on the road shuts off its existence altogether, as if it had never been. This passage is repeated again and again, until the weight of these places lies upon the memory like a heavy cloak of hopelessness. To observe a country's destitution is not to condemn it, but there is always something about poverty that demands an explanation. You realize that it is not the peasants, alternating between simple leisure and cheerful industry, who will supply one.

We rounded a bend, and a river came into view. There was the inevitable ferry crossing with its motionless line of waiting trucks. The traffic had been scarce, however, and they numbered only a dozen or so. The ferry, made small by the distance, was nearing the opposite bank, but it would soon be returning. We pulled into line to wait.

The Chinese are a patient people, accepting the lines that their numbers and their poverty and their bureaucrats create with good-natured submission. Here the drivers had alighted from their parked trucks and, squatting close to the fenders for the sliver of shadow that they threw, seemed to have gone into meditation. Ming, too, enjoyed the respite from the rugged roads, and possessing the enviable ability of the peasant to go to sleep at any time and in any position, he promptly exercised it. For myself, I would have preferred the cooling breeze that motion offered. Stopped, the heat made it impossible to sit in the van, and I did not have the faculty of squatting on my haunches for long lengths of time. It cut off the circulation in my legs. So I stood, watching the approaching ferry, straining to count the number of trucks on board.

There were only six. I groaned inwardly. The ferry was miniscule and it would take at least one, possibly two more round trips before we would get across. In a passenger van, I could have gone right to the head of the line upon arrival. I had already committed myself to the line, though, and now felt bound by its order.

A feeble-looking old woman and a small but sturdy-looking boy came slowly up the line of trucks hawking icesticks, a kind of Chinese Popsicle. Theirs was a fine division of labor. The boy carried the oversized thermos bottle, managing it well even though it was fully half as high as he was, while the old woman, whose shrill voice was still in fine fettle, cried out "Icesticks for sale, icesticks for sale." The drivers ignored the pair, but this purgatorial waiting in the sun had made me thirsty and I motioned them over.

"What kind of icesticks are you selling, auntie?"

"Red bean icesticks," she cackled happily, sensing a sale. "Three fen each." This concoction of mashed red beans frozen in sugar water was not a favorite of mine, but I bought one anyway to quench my thirst. I finished it in a few bites and had another, then a third. Realizing that she had stumbled upon a gold mine, the old woman gave up crying her wares and hovered protectively around me as I ate, telling me how she was teaching the boy, her grandson, to make change even though he was only seven and not in school yet. Soon he would be able to hawk icesticks at this crossing on his own.

He already seemed qualified to me. There was nothing childish in the way that he deftly spun open the top of the thermos, quickly pulling out an icestick and clapping the top back on before the cold escaped, and no hesitation in the act of taking my ten-fen note and giving me seven fen in change. His grandmother had trained him well, impressing on him the importance of what he was doing. He was all business, and his gravity seemed incongruous in one so young.

"A little capitalist weed," Ming, who had awakened to regard the pair, mocked gently as soon as they were out of earshot. No one familiar with China's recent history would have missed the referent. The late Chairman Mao had devoted his life to the eradication of commercial activity, metaphorically described as the uprooting of "capitalist weeds." This little boy, born not long before the Chairman had died, and learning to sell before he could read, personified the resurgent spirit of entrepreneurship in China, and the abjectness of Mao's failure.

The ferry docked: the drivers climbed into their cabs, creeped up by half-a-dozen vehicles, and dismounted again, resuming their squat meditation. It was very hot.

The nearness of the river led me down to its bank. I took off my sandals and walked in the shallows, my feet sinking deeply into the cold mud underneath. It was a very un-Chinese thing to do. Most peasants don't know how to swim, and give rivers and lakes a wide berth. Tales of water ghosts who lurk in the deep waiting to pull down and drown the unwarry further discourage them, as does the knowledge that a chill caught during the heat of a tropical summer can easily be deadly. But to

me the cool, rushing waters held nothing more than relief, and soon I
had shed my shirt and gone swimming again. This peculiar behavior
roused the other drivers from their drowsy stupor, and they gathered
along the bank to gawk as I churned water, probably taking bets on the
likelihood of my imminent demise.

I paid for that swim with a tropical fever that seized upon me suddenly an hour later. My neck and shoulders began to ache mercilessly,
and the jolting road became a torture. Ming stopped in the next county
town we passed and disappeared into a herbal apothecary, promising to
purchase some medicines to reduce the pain and fever.

I had been dozing off in the van when all at once I heard a man's
voice bellow: "All illegally parked vehicles must be moved immediately." I opened sticky eyes to see a policeman with a bullhorn standing
some twenty yards away in front of the county transportation inspection station. This is an organization that is a highway patrol and a department of motor vehicles all in one. For the first time I noticed that
in front of the station, at the intersection of the only two paved roads in
town, there had been erected a "no parking" sign. These are rare in
county towns, where there are usually too few vehicles in use for it to
matter where they park. The sign was being totally ignored by drivers
and I counted, in additon to our van, no fewer than eight trucks within
the prohibited fifty-meter radius of the sign. The man with the bullhorn
had begun coming down the street, shouting as he went: "All drivers
return to your vehicles and move them at once. This is an order." As he
continued his summons, two drivers sauntered out, got into their trucks,
and drove away. They had not appeared to be in any particular hurry.
The number of illegally parked trucks was thus reduced to six. The official disappeared inside the station and I thought the episode over.

But no. Five minutes later he reemerged from the station, minus the
bullhorn but carrying a large screwdriver. He walked over to the nearest
truck and proceeded to remove the screws holding its license plate, then
slipped the plates into his pocket. He worked quickly, and soon had the
license plates of all six offending vehicles off and in his pocket. In the
place where each license had been, he wrote in chalk in heavy block
characters: "License has been ticketed." I was sure that the returning
drivers would be taken aback by their missing license plates. It could not

have been a common occurrence. The official had used the wrong character for the word ''ticket.''

The van was passed over with nothing more than a queer glance, it being a type of vehicle that is little seen in inland China. The humor and tension of the episode had temporarily cleared my head of the obscurantist fever. I began to survey my surroundings with more interest.

I saw two youths, whose swarthy features, thick hands, and wide feet stamped them as peasants, walking closely together under an umbrella that the taller one held high to screen them from the sun. They were identically dressed in plastic sunglasses, plastic sandals, new white shirts, and baggy pants. The only clue to their sex was their sandals. The taller one's sandals were black, the shorter one's pink. They were a newly married peasant couple from a remote mountain village who had dressed in their wedding finery for the one-day journey to this county town. The woman seemed excited, as well she might be, for she had never left her mountain fastness before, and years might pass before she would again.

There next appeared on the street an apparition of a man—I am guessing at the sex—with his hair falling tangled and filthy down to his shoulders, his feet bare and black, and his clothes so tattered and encrusted with dirt that they looked as if they would soon simply rot off of his body altogether. As he slouched along, the crowd parted in front of him as if by magic, and he made his way undisturbed. I soon found out why. As he passed the van, it was invaded with an odor of such foulness that I gagged. Yet it was his burned and blackened face that disturbed me most of all. It wore the vacant, helpless expression of a newborn infant, and I knew that he was badly retarded. I had seen similar cases in the Delta. The retarded and the insane are the private burden of the parents who bore them, and if the latter die before their offspring, these poor creatures are often cast out by less sympathetic siblings or more distant relatives to make their way in life as best they can.

The bitter herbal concoction that Ming came back with made me drowsy, and the next couple of hours on the road I wanted nothing more than to sleep. I found it impossible. Each time I would begin to drift off, my nodding head would be thrown against the window post by a bump in the road. Then I would start upright, staring blankly out at the road, aware of little more than a ribbon of blurred brown in a wilderness of green and the pain in my head. I would resolve to remain awake but, perspiring, feverish, and terribly weak, I began to doze off again within a minute. It was frustrating, in a somnolent sort of way. I could feel my head lolling to one side, but in this paralyzed state between sleeping and waking, I could not summon the strength to hold it upright. I could only observe helplessly as my head swung closer and closer to the window post, finally colliding with it once again. Whether it was because of these repeated concussions or the efficacy of Chinese herbal medicines I know not, but two hours later, as we approached the outskirts of Liuchow, my head cleared, and the fever left me as suddenly as it had come.

The city straddled the Liu River, which formed the dividing line between the government offices and officials' quarters on the north bank of the river, and the factories and workers' dormitories on the south bank. In contrast to other greying Chinese cities I had seen, which looked for the most part as if the clock had stopped three decades ago when the People's Liberation Army arrived, the city of Liuchow had wide boulevards and a large number of new, if heavy and unattractive, office and apartment buildings. Ming wasn't long in telling me why. During the Cultural Revolution the workers, most of whom had belonged to the same Red Guard faction, had engaged in armed warfare with the officials, who had joined another. It was class warfare with a vengeance. "They fought with tanks and howitzers, and the city center was leveled," Ming recalled. "They had to rebuild it from the ground up in the seventies. That's why it looks almost new." In a sense, Liuchow had been lucky. San Francisco had an earthquake, Chicago a fire, and Liuchow a civil war, and the cities that emerged from the ruins were more pleasing places to live than they had been.

Pleasing, that is, except for two things.

Ming did not recall which faction had come out on top in the ferocious fighting, but I could tell that the victors had wanted to leave no doubt where their loyalties lay. I had grown used to the government graffiti that bedecked public buildings in China, but never before had I seen so much in one place. The city existed as an exhibition of quotations from Chairman Mao. Every new construction had a famous saying of the Chairman carved in concrete or painted in red alongside its entranceway. The stanchions of the bridges across the Liu River sang out the eulogistic hope that "May Mao Tse-tung live for ten thousand years." And at the epicenter of the city that had seen such upheavals in his name, a thirty-foot-high statue of the man himself stood. I have often wondered since how much of this political kitsch will survive the Teng years. I suspect not very much.

Few trucks or cars plied the wide boulevards, but again and again we encountered men wearing the conical hats of coolies who were pulling little carts to and fro. They looked like rickshaws except that where the passenger would have sat there was instead a small tank, painted a dark green. From the tangy, umistakable odor that marked the carts' passage, I realized that they were the modern-day equivalent of the honey buckets in which the city's human manure had once departed the city for use on peasant fields. I seem to remember the streets of Liuchow as crawling with such vehicles, but my memory may be playing me false. It is the nature of this article of commerce that it makes an impression out of proportion to its actual bulk.

After a bath and a brief nap in the city's recently completed tourist hotel, it was time to explore the city on foot. My goal was a collection of medieval temples and their surrounding grounds that had been walled off and converted into a "people's park." I had wanted to take a look inside, but couldn't get past the gate. It was only 5:30 P.M. and the park was not supposed to close until 6:00, but the ticket seller refused to sell me a ticket, saying that it was too near to closing time. "We don't like to let anyone in after about 5:15. It's easier to clear the park that way." It seemed to me a strange way to run a people's park, but I was soon to understand the source of their difficulties.

I had scarcely walked a score of paces away from the park entrance when out popped a small, dirty boy, hand outstretched. His eyes looked at me in a wild, defiant, and decidedly un-Chinese way but he said nothing. Nor did he need to. His gesture spoke for itself. Ming didn't even break stride (he told me later that he was used to beggars) but I was stopped in my tracks by my miniature confronter. He was about four feet high, dressed in faded peasant blues a size too small, and could have used a bath.

"How much do you want?" I asked gently.

"Money," he said in heavily accented Mandarin, establishing the parameters of our conversation. His features were rigid as he spoke, and

I decided that it wasn't insolence but fear that I read there. Of course he was afraid. He had not expected when he stepped out in my path to be facing a foreign devil.

"Yes, but how much money?" I queried. I was glad that it was nearly dark. I had found boys begging in Canton but I had not been able to talk to them because it had been daylight, and my questions had drawn crowds, frightening the children into silence or flight. Here people on their way home from work simply hurried by. I had a chance to unravel the mystery of these small panhandlers.

"Do you want one fen, two fen, five fen, ten fen, twenty fen, fifty fen, or one yuan?" He stared at me fixedly as I upped the stakes, and I stopped for fear of making him speechless.

"People mostly give me one fen," he said, beginning to open up. "I can buy a mantou [steamed roll] for five fen."

Out of the corner of my eye, I noticed three other gamins edging over toward us out of the dark recess of an entryway. They were similarly dressed but looked a little younger, perhaps eight or nine.

"Now you're in for it," Ming grinned mirthlessly. "You'll have to feed the whole gang." He had seen what I had suspected, that they were all together.

"How many of you are there?" I asked the first boy.

"We are four," he replied. "All from the same commune." And then, to bring the conversation back to the heart of the matter, he added: "We have not eaten today."

"I will give you money, but first you must tell me where you come from." He named a commune, but it was lost in his accent and the homophones of Chinese. I asked him to write it.

"I cannot." He was abashed. "It is a complicated character. But I can write my name." I handed him my notebook, and he scrawled in large, childish characters Wang Er-nung—"Wang Second Farmer." Like most of the children in his village, he had attended only two years of school. He told me that his parents were still in the village, as were his older brother and younger sister. He had been sent away several weeks ago when the weather had become warm because there wasn't enough food. The "spring famine" had begun in the village as last year's crops were exhausted. He could go back in a month at the time of the sweet potato harvest.

"Why were you sent and not your older brother?" I asked, thinking of the irony of his second-rate name.

"Father says that he is big enough to help on the land. Anyway, people give less food and money to older children." He may have been a functional illiterate, but he was streetwise.

The younger children were less forward than Second Farmer, whom they clustered around and seemed to look up to as a leader, but their stories were similar. They were here in the city begging because there was nothing to eat at home.

"I will give you money," I said, "but you must promise to share it."

"Yes," Second Farmer said eagerly. "We are brothers." Out of their common misfortune had sprung strong bonds, a fraternity of castoff children.

I gave them one yuan. Their eyes widened as they saw it (as did Ming's). It was enough to buy them food for several days. They warmed to the discussion now. I had revealed myself as a friend by my assistance to them in their exile.

"Where do you pass the night?"

Second Farmer led me to the darkened entranceway out of which his friends had appeared. There were a couple of tattered bamboo mats laid up against the doors. They slept huddled together under the partial shelter of the recessed entrance on the mats. It was warm enough during the day, but the nights were chilly, and the dew that descended at 3:00 A.M. dampened everything out-of-doors. "We get chased away in the morning. The gatekeeper comes to work at dawn."

"What about the police?"

"We run from the police," one of the younger boys piped up.

"Why?"

This time Second Farmer answered. The police didn't want them in the city. If caught, they were trucked or carted out of the city and warned not to come back. They came back anyway because it was hard to beg in the countryside. "We have been caught twice. The police beat us. We change sleeping places every few nights so the local police station will not know where we are sleeping." And with a hint of bravado: "They will not catch us again."

It was now completely dark, with only a few dim lights from the buildings across the street to give illumination to the little shadows with whom I was conversing. The recess that gave them shelter was dark, like a cave, and faintly foreboding. I wished them good night, and there was nothing to save this simple greeting from mockery except their innocence.

I inwardly reproached their parents for sending their children away to suffer like this. Yet conditions in some of the villages I had seen were little better than those faced by these boys. And in the high mountains, where I had not yet been, it was the "hungry season," those painful, recurring periods described by the Chinese peasant as "When the green [the new harvest] and the yellow [the old grain] do not meet." It made a kind of cruel sense to risk an unproductive child to the road, and use the food saved to fuel the productive in their efforts to grow another crop, staving off starvation for another season.

If I was angry at their parents, I was livid at the state, which, rather than take responsibility for these waifs, bullied them and ran them out of town. Another Chinese saying came to mind: "To be poor at home is not really poverty, but to be poor and on the road can kill you." I wondered how many of these children, without proper food and shelter, would survive the summer. And how many of their deaths would be caused by the authorities, who kept them from sleeping in the parks with high walls and entrance fees, who turned them out of whatever shelter they were able to improvise, and who harassed them by day, forcing them to keep out of sight and beg silently, sticking out a grubby hand to isolated passersby? They were afraid to call attention to themselves. If they, like beggers in the "Old" China, were to cry out in as loud and piteous a voice as possible, "Have a kind heart—a few pennies—feed a starving person," they would quickly attract the attention of the public security cadres, and would be beaten and driven out of town for "undermining the socialist order."

In the official rhetoric the police served the people, unemployment was low, and hunger had been abolished. For those fortunate enough to live in the cities, these claims might be valid. To them the state presents a paternal face, demanding total obedience but meeting their basic needs for food, clothing, and shelter. However, for the vast numbers of rural Chinese who live outside these socialist enclaves, promises have not been kept.[2] For them the state has only exhortations to self-reliance, and stern warnings against migrating to the cities. And those who out of desperation come anyway, like these hungry children, were in their rags easy to identify and drive out again. To the urban powers-that-be, stray peasant children weren't people, they were intruders on a complex system of rationed food, clothing, and shelter that guaranteed urban order and control. There were no ration coupons allotted to them, no work or housing assignments reserved for them, and so they didn't exist. How brutal that children should be treated this way just because as peasants they are not registered in the cities.

The Liuchow Hotel for foreign guests was typical of the structures that sprang up all over China after Peking opened the door to large-scale tourism in 1978. Twelve stories high, elevators and bathroom fixtures imported from Hong Kong, towels, soap, and food obtained locally, and empty. Apparently no one had considered whether any of the tourists expected to pour into China would come to Liuchow, a smokestack city in South China with little to recommend it to the tourist except a history of violence and a large central park that closed at dusk, and no means of access except the rail line that stopped here enroute from Kweilin in the north to Nanning in the south. Of the hotel's three-hundred-odd rooms, all but ten were empty, and the manager, a nervous little man desperate to generate some revenue, pressed me to take a twelfth-floor suite at ninety yuan a night. I settled instead for an ordinary room at one-third the price.

The dining room was enormous, taking up half a floor, and filled with banquet-sized tables each of which could easily seat twelve. When we walked in, there were exactly three customers, a group of young women from Hong Kong. Hearing familiar accents made me long for a little company. I decided to go over and introduce myself.

"You can't do that," Ming remonstrated. "You don't even know them."

[2] While average grain consumption in China fell by 3.2 per cent between 1957 and 1978, not all groups were equally affected. Peasants were eating 5.9 per cent less grain, while workers and officials were eating 10.5 per cent more. See Nicholas Lardy, *Agriculture in China's Modern Economic Development* (Cambridge: Cambridge University Press, 1983), p. 157.

But they were friendly and invited us to join them, and for the second time I saw Ming's veneer of cynical sophistication crack. He was a man of the world where other villagers were concerned, but he behaved like a rustic in the presence of these young women from Hong Kong. He avoided looking directly at them, laughed too often and too loud, and said nothing except for occasional whispered asides to me.

The girls told me that, no, they weren't visiting relatives, they were on their way to Nanning, the capital of Kwangsi, in the south.

"They must come from wealthy capitalist families," Ming said for my ears only.

But they didn't. They were ordinary working girls, who had recently been laid off by a Hong Kong textile factory and had decided to take a trip before looking for another job.

"Unemployed?" Ming's voice was an urgent whisper. "How can they afford to travel?"

The girls had come to Liuchow because the city had been a place of refuge from the invading Japanese for one of their fathers during World War II. But they had found little to do—they had visited the park that afternoon and had been unimpressed—and were leaving for Nanning by train on the morrow.

After dinner we walked about the hotel, Ming trailing along behind, and discovered a tiny gift shop occupying an out-of-the-way corner. Expecting to find the usual tourist junk—ashtrays, bamboo fans, postcards, and the like—we were instead confronted with stacks of Chinese fireworks. There were firecrackers, cherry bombs, miniature rockets, Roman candles, and pinwheels of every size and shape. It made for a fascinating display, though hardly seemed the sort of thing that tourists would buy. I got the story out of the clerk. Liuchow, it so happened, was an important center for the manufacture of fireworks. When the directive came down instructing Chinese cities on the tourist track to open shops selling "famous local products," the local lead-and-cardboard bureaucrats had followed it to the letter. They had set up this tiny shop to sell Liuchow's "famous" fireworks.

On impulse I bought an armful of fireworks and headed for the roof, Ming and the three girls in tow. If it was legal to buy the fireworks, surely it was also legal to fire them off. The fireworks were good. The firecrackers burst with convincing bangs, the rockets shot up high in the night sky trailing orange flames, and the Roman candles burst into spheres of colored light that hung in the clear night sky like giant Christmas tree ornaments. Ming helped me ignite the fuses, and the girls laughed and clapped at each new display, but I soon tired of the frivolity. I still had to write up my notes about the homeless boys before I could sleep.

CHAPTER FIVE

Into the High Country

Iт was easier to check into the Liuchow Hotel than it was to check out. After I paid my room charge, the girl behind the counter mumbled something about getting a stamp, and disappeared out the main entrance to the hotel. "She's going to the public security office down the street to get your travel permit stamped," the other clerk apologized.

"Isn't that normally done in the hotel?" I queried.

"Yes," she replied, "it's just that we haven't been issued our official stamp yet. We have only been open three months."

I had a bad feeling about this turn of events. Anytime you tangle with the bureaucracy in China you are in for a delay—sometimes hours, sometimes days—and public security was especially notorious in this regard. I would have sunk into a chair in dismay, except that there were no chairs in the huge, empty lobby ("The furniture we ordered hasn't arrived yet"). After circling aimlessly in the lobby for a while, I went out and sat in the van. The minutes ticked slowly by. The sun climbed higher, dissipating the morning freshness. I had wanted to reach the mountains before the day's heat came upon us.

An hour passed, then another. Finally I saw the clerk coming down the street, walking in that bold, manlike fashion given to Chinese women in full stride by their baggy trousers. She handed me my travel permit and apologized for the delay. Ming started the engine.

Just then a young Chinese woman came running out the main entrance of the hotel, pigtails flying. I recognized her as the attendant of the floor we had stayed on the previous night.

"Please return the facecloth that you took from the room," she said between gasps, for she was out of breath.

The set of towels in the room had been embossed with the characters "Liuchow Hotel" and, wanting a souvenir of my visit (fireworks did not seem an appropriate or safe memento), I had packed away the smallest. It was a facecloth, a foot-square hank of cheap terrycloth, worth perhaps twenty fen at local prices. I had paid fifty-two yuan for rooms for Ming and myself. Now here the attendant was, demanding the facecloth back.

"Can I pay you for it?" I started to hand her a one-yuan bill, about five times what I judged the facecloth to be worth. She waved away the money.

"You don't understand." She was practically wringing her hands as she spoke. "I am responsible for all of the towels on my floor. It's very hard to order new towels, and we don't have any extra." It was obvious that the facecloth meant more to her than it did to me, so I dug it out of my bags and returned it to her.

The sun was high in the cloudless sky by the time we were finally on the road, and the humid air rushing in through the open window of the van had lost its power to cool. Today was going to be a scorcher. Still, there were compensations. The brilliant sunshine brought out the strong primary colors of South China to an eye-watering intensity. The splendid greens of the foliage, the reddish ochres of the soil, the blue of the sky, the ribbon of red that was the road itself, all burned themselves into the retina. And more clearly than ever before we saw the prosperity of suburban villages like those we had visited in Kweilin give way over the next hour to the dogged self-sufficiency of more distant communes.

"The further away from Liuchow—or any large city—you go, the poorer people are." Ming had been prompted to speak by the sight of an old man astride a water buffalo. "Here some people still have bikes, but it's too far to ride to Liuchow so they have to be content with what they can sell at the local market. They have few places to go. They live simpler lives, like their ancestors did. We will travel further in a day than most of these people have ever traveled in their entire lives.''

As we passed out of this commune whose residents still rode water buffaloes, Ming pointed out that it, too, was called Liberation. He gave me one of his secret smiles, as if to say that it would take more than the installation of a ''progressive'' name to improve the lives of the people who lived there. It was hard to engage in a charitable self-censorship of my thoughts with Ming around. He found the contrast between these desolate places and the desperate optimism of their names grimly amusing as well.

Thirst made us stop in Ishan, a county seat about sixty miles west of Liuchow. A couple of cold beers would have been my preference, but I knew there would be none available in a town this small. Ming voted for hot tea, the favorite summer drink of the Chinese, but the only restaurant in town was closed. A local soda parlor filled with morose-looking youths was our only option. I paid thirty fen for two bottles of soda pop, cheap to me but a goodly part of a day's wages for those present. The county pride, a heavily carbonated syrupy-salty liquid with an off-citrus flavor, was just bearable ice-cold, and we each had a second bottle. But I vetoed Ming's suggestion that we purchase a six-pack for the road, sure that when it reached room temperature it would be gagging. The outward glumness of the patrons was, I decided, a reflection of their inner dilemma: Should they slowly nurse their expensive drinks to make them last as long as possible, or should they quickly quaff them before they had a chance to warm up?

I have had reasonably good carbonated beverages in China. That of the Delta county I lived in was a very palatable orange-flavored drink. In open competition it would have won hands down over this and the other inland soda pops I sampled. But in China, with its bias toward planning and against marketing, open competition is precisely what is not permitted. How much simpler to decree that each county shall have a beverage plant, whose product shall be sold only within that county. If that state-awarded monopoly meant that the sober youths sitting in the soda parlor had a choice between drinking an inferior brand or going thirsty, well, it was a small price to pay for economic order.

Western businessmen have long spun wild fantasies about the China market. A nineteenth-century English cotton-mill owner is supposed to have mused: "If I could only persuade the Chinese to add twelve inches to the tails of their shirts, I could keep my mills going for five hundred years." In 1980 a representative of a large American chemical firm was being only slightly less fanciful when he declared: "We realize that China's purchasing power is limited, but if we can only sell one aspirin to every Chinese, that's a hell of a lot of aspirin." The problem with this view is that for foreign firms to be able to sell aspirins or anything else to the Chinese public, Peking will have to first give up its lucrative monopoly position in the Chinese market. This is extremely unlikely to happen. The handful of apparent exceptions to this rule, as when Coca-Cola signed an agreement with Peking to build a bottling company in China, usually look different up close. In the case of Coca-Cola, the central planners allowed the company in the country for the sole purpose of selling its product to visiting tourists, who, it was wisely anticipated, would have trouble getting used to the local brews. Coke was available only in the urban hotels, restaurants, and special stores patronized by foreign visitors. I could no more have purchased a can of Coke in the interior of China than I could have purchased a bottle of Tylenol.

The road started climbing as soon as we left Ishan, turning and turning again, gaining altitude. There was an odd thing about this road. When it came to a mountain it would either skirt it, clinging precariously to its side, or it would coil itself up into a series of switchbacks and mount it. But it would not tunnel it. Indeed, we had traveled hundreds of miles through terrain that ranged from the rugged to the merely hilly, and the road had not once plunged into the earth or bulldozed through obstacles. Rather, it ran lightly over the ground with a kind of exaggerated respect for it, finessing even the smallest hummocks, like an outsized nature trail. It was the kind of flesh-and-blood road that peasants armed with picks and wheelbarrows would construct, and it made slow going. We had come only about 120 miles all told the day before, a stone's throw by the freewheeling standards of America's superhighways, and would likely not even roll up that distance today.

Doggedly twisting and turning around hills, occasionally dipping through valleys but never giving up its upward progress for long, the road continued. Change was continuous but largely invisible, a gradual sloughing away of the man-made order of the midlands. For a while rice terraces staggered up the hills after us, but then, as if exhausted by the climb, gave way to tasseled stands of spindly corn and low green spreads of sweet potatoes. Then even these carefully cultivated patches grew smaller and more scattered in a landscape increasingly dominated by the lush anarchy of tropical vegetation.

We had entered a wilderness, yet it was far from unpopulated. Even in this rough country, every curve brought another hamlet into view. This was land that had not always been wanted. A thousand years ago during the Tang and Sung dynasties, when great waves of migration from the North China heartland had surged southward, the area had been scorned by settlers bound for more fertile lowlands east and south. Only after the Portuguese had introduced the New World crops of maize and sweet potatoes to China in the sixteenth century could peasants survive on these rocky slopes in any numbers, for only then could they feed themselves. But it had obviously been hardscrabble all the way. Visible from the road were the smallest plots, the lowest, most primitive thatched huts I had yet seen.

The sense of traveling back in time that had temporarily abated in Liuchow now reasserted itself. It did not help that we lost the provincial radio station shortly after entering the mountains, leaving nothing on the AM and FM bands except the crackle of static. I did not miss the high, singsong voice of the announcer reading Party directives and government news bulletins, nor the martial music and revolutionary songs. But one more link with the modern world had been snapped.

Had I needed evidence that somewhere outside this Chinese Appalachia radio stations still broadcast and were being received, that the advancements of the last hundred years had not somehow been negated, I could have switched over to the shortwave bands. Not so the Chinese. Radios sold in the PRC do not have shortwave bands, and those imported that do are disabled by customs officials. It was less important to the Chinese state that isolated areas like this be in touch with the larger world than that China be sealed off from outside influences like the Voice of America or, worse yet, the Republic of China broadcasts from Taiwan. The airwaves were owned by the state. Not that it made any difference. One had but to look at the niggardly extent of the tillage, the short, uneven rows of spindly maize, to know that the tillers would not own any radios at all.

We came to a high massif which the road climbed in a seemingly endless series of switchbacks, winding back down the other side in the same dizzying fashion into a tiny valley, really little more than a canyon. Its narrow floor was a checkerboard of small, interlocking paddy fields. By the shoulder of the road, not far from a little hamlet, a small group of peasants were working a pile of compost.

A swarm of invisible biting midges descended on us as soon as we alighted from the van, gnats so small that you couldn't see them or even hear them buzz until they bit you. Even insect repellent didn't help, and we stood slapping ourselves awkwardly, unlike the leathery-skinned locals whom the gnats didn't seem to bother. Hoping to escape my tiny tormentors, I set off in the direction of the hamlet. Ming followed, passing out cigarettes to the men we passed in what had become our standard ritual of friendship. No one said a word.

Up close, the huts were meaner than I had realized from the road, and I mentally noted their similarity to the shacks I had seen in Mexican slums. Those had been poor habitations, built of rusty tin and tattered cardboard, the roof weighted down against the furies of tropical storms by an assortment of broken bricks and old tires, TV aerials angling awkwardly overhead. There had been dogs lazing in doorways, fat women in old acrylics and secondhand nylons, dirty urchins in torn sweaters and pants about to wear out at the knees, and pigs rooting in the garbage that lay about. Those slum dwellers had been denizens of the fringe, constructing their lives out of the leavings of modern industrial society.

But it was apparent that the Chinese peasants here did not merely live on the fringes of an industrial economy, they were lost to it entirely. Their village was an organic thing, of a piece with its stone-age landscape. Their huts had walls of local earth, roofs of local thatch, and doors of local bamboo. No antennas poked out of the thatch overhead, and no bicycles were parked under the frayed eaves. There were no dogs, for there was no surplus food to feed them. ("One dog eats as much rice as a ten-year-old-child," Ming explained later.) There were no pigs, for there was no garbage for them to root in. There were only people, dressed in plain cotton clothes made to last, like the peasants themselves, from season to season. The Mexican slums were squalid, yet at the same time were somehow energized by the nearness of the city and the vigor of the children. Here in the high mountains there was only destitution, quiet and utter. This was mirrored in the faces of the peasants, young and old alike, who had stopped talking and moved together as I approached, as deer will seek the safety of the herd when they sense a foreign presence.

They were a tiny folk, small-statured and fine-boned. Village men in the Delta had been generally a half a head shorter than me. These villagers gave away a full head, and the women more. It was as if their growth had been stunted by their tiny huts—the way goldfish never grow larger than their bowl. A more prosaic explanation was that they suffered from long-term malnutrition which had affected their adult height and weight.

Because of the various food rations and subsidies given to urban residents, chronic malnutrition in the cities has dropped to low levels. In the countryside, though, it remains a problem. One study which compared urban children with children from relatively prosperous suburban communes found that low height for age, known as ''stunting,'' was three times as common among rural populations and that low weight for age was eight times as common.[1] In this high mountain village, the affliction seemed general.

At first I thought that these quiet peasants may have been made uneasy by my size, but as they continued to stare at me, unease and something approaching wonder mingling on their faces, another hypothesis began to form in my mind. They had taken cigarettes from Ming readily enough, but now when I stretched out my hand with the same offering they backed away, like suspicious children who had been warned not to accept candy from strangers. I studied their reaction and grew sure of it. They had never seen a white man before.

I was certainly not the first Caucasion to come this way. This hamlet was after all on the main route, such that it was, connecting Kwangsi and Kweichow, a road that had been opened in the 1920s. Members of American military-assistance groups may have jeeped by here during World War II and been spotted by a villager or two. Perhaps a priest had been active in the county town—there had been a number of French Catholic missions and outstations in Kwangsi early in the twentieth century—and been seen by some of the older men. But these and other

[1] China: Socialist Economic Development, 9 vols. (Washington, D.C.: International Bank for Reconstruction and Development, 1981), pp. 14–16.

foreigners vanished with the coming of Communist rule in 1949, and in these hills there were no movies, no TV, and no magazines or newspapers to keep their existence unquestioned. There was one thing certain: No one here under the age of thirty-five had ever before come upon a foreigner. They might have heard tales that the world was home to people who did not have black hair and bronze skin, but that knowledge had not been real until, on that road where trucks rarely passed and never stopped, a metal box with wheels had appeared.

I was wondering what to do when a cadre dressed in the blue trousers and white shirt of his class came walking up the road. If this man had never seen a foreigner before, you couldn't tell it from his open, even assertive manner, which formed a study in contrasts with the behavior of the quiet people he led. As a Communist Party member and returning People's Liberation Army soldier, he had been assigned to the post of brigade head fifteen years ago. But if I had expected him to be an apologist for the state's policies toward the people of these mountains, I was mistaken. He had been born here. They were his people.

"How large is the brigade?"

"About eight hundred people. One hundred fifty of them live in this valley." He made a sweep of his hand outward. The gesture reminded me of Ming. "They are the La-chin Team, the 'Pull Forward' Team. They are called that because they divide about four hundred pounds of unhusked grain a year per worker. This is the highest of all the eight teams in the brigade. Most of the teams are in the mountains and don't have any paddy."

Unhusked grain loses about 30 percent of its weight in the husking, so that able-bodied members of this team received only 280 pounds of rice a year, well below the minimum of 330 pounds of husked grain set by Peking. They depended on small hillside plots of sweet potatoes and corn to make up the difference. And what about "in the mountains"?

"Mountain teams eat boiled sweet potatoes or corn porridge all year round. Even here we mostly eat rice porridge with sweet potatoes mixed in. We only get about two hundred pounds of unhusked rice per mou [about one-sixth of an acre] because we have no fertilizer and no irrigation. We have to depend upon rainfall."

"Are things better now than they were before?" I asked. I was hoping to draw him out on the differences between life now and life before the coming of the Communists, but he answered with a more recent time period in mind.

"Things are a lot better now than they were," he began. "During the Cultural Revolution the authorities made us plant two rice crops a year. The first one was stunted by the cold because we had to plant it too early, while the second never matured because it was planted too late. Some years we had no grain at all. We were eating bitterness."

My question had gone awry. I knew that the Cultural Revolution (1966–1976) was universally hated in the cities and in the Delta, but I had not anticipated that it would be so bitterly etched in the memory of these mountain people that it superseded all other bases for comparison. At the same time, his answer suggested that things had improved somewhat since the state relaxed its control. I decided to pursue that.

"How much cash do you distribute to your collective members each year?"

"How can we earn cash?" He was still smiling, but I could tell that I had pushed one of his buttons. His words came tumbling out. "We have only our two hundred mou. We grow just enough to feed ourselves. We have no grain to sell to the state, no cash crops, no brigade enterprises. Even the mountains here don't belong to us. There is a lot of wood in the mountains here, but the state started a forestry preserve twenty years ago and we are forbidden to cut down any trees."

"What about the modernization program, won't it help?" Later, when I better understood the hopeless situation that these mountain peasants, and others like them, were in, I regreted asking this question. It must have sounded either naive or mocking.

He told me they had no hand tractors, no bicycles, no electric pumps, no radios, no electricity, and only one wind-up clock that he had purchased while in the military. Nevertheless, he deadpanned, we will have a television set in the year 2000.

At that some of the peasants tittered. I wondered if any of them had ever seen a TV set. Throughout this conversation the other peasants— and they had grown to some twenty by the time we parted—stood apart, as if emphasizing the gulf separating them from their spokesman. He had been out of the valley, and had visited other parts of China. They had not. I reflected that it was probably harder for him than it was for the others. After all, he understood what the world outside of his valley was like. For the rest of them, the few dozen square miles of the commune still constituted the known world; their vision was still limited by their fateful involvement with their own valley.

"The people in these mountains live in the age of the primitives," Ming said when we were back on the road. If I had thought Ming was going to engage in his usual cheery chauvinism about how much wealthier his Delta people were than the locals, I was dead wrong. Instead of his usual humorous contempt, there was a new note in his voice, a shame that people in his country could live so poorly. "The social environment [a common phrase in China] won't allow them to develop. They have no science, industry, or education. They are forced to stay in place and grow a few grains of rice. They are given no fertilizer. All they have is their own shit. It's a joke to think that they can modernize."

The afternoon bore out his observations, revealing these mountains as a place of stony natural certainties and infrangible state laws. I continued to stop in the villages and talk to people, but each interview was briefer than the last, as I abandoned one topic after another. It made no sense to ask about electricity in the absence of power lines. It seemed pointless to ask about the possible mechanization of field work after one team head spit on the ground and allowed that his real problem was keeping enough hoes in repair to work the team's sweet-potato plots, and another told me that the commune five miles away had purchased a tractor ("iron ox") a few years ago, but it had broken down that same year and there was no one to repair it. I stopped asking questions about how many village children finished elementary school and went on to high school after finding out that many of the smaller hamlets had no schools at all, and that even the larger ones had only a "lower primary school" consisting of grades one through four. Often the only upper primary schools were in the larger brigades and the commune seat. I abandoned queries about the local collective medical program after I learned that it did not exist, and could not exist, because these mountain peasants did not participate in the cash economy and could not pay the premiums, and that a brigade was lucky if it had a single barefoot doctor—a villager with three months of training in basic hygiene and first aid. The state of both the local health-care and birth-control programs seemed fairly well summed up by a middle-aged man who told me that everyone wants three or four children because "children have a thin fate,'' meaning that they often die, an observation confirmed by the packs of anemic-looking young children and toddlers standing about in each collection of huts I visited. In the end I was reduced to asking about the basics, the production and consumption of food, and found that the peasants in these mountains were consuming in grains and root crops a total of not more than 1,500 calories a day. This seemed low to me at the time, but it was only after I left China that I was able to check it against an objective standard. The U.N. Food and Agricultural Organization defines malnourishment as less than 1,600 calories a day.

It was in these villages that I began to hear the women speaking a silibant, hissing tongue that was quite unlike any Chinese dialect I knew. ''Chwang language,'' Ming offered without hesitation, even counting to ten for my benefit, as many a North American can stumble to ten in Spanish. ''Many Han men in this area have taken Chwang wives because their brideprice is lower,'' Ming explained. ''It can cost hundreds of yuan in cash and presents before a Han Chinese family will let you marry their daughter. Here you can buy a young Chwang woman for a hundred yuan or less.''

That was my introduction to the Chwang, the largest Chinese minority, estimated to be some twelve million strong. Although there were Chwang in each of the surrounding provinces of Kweichow, Kwangtung, and Yunnan, most of this number were concentrated in western Kwangsi. This was the very region that we were now entering, and it was not long before nearly all the people we saw were Chwang. The women were easy to recognize as Chwang, even from a distance, for they all wore traditional dress—black pants and tops, white scarves, and blue, high-necked aprons with a winged silver brooch pinned on the apron near the throat. The men were not, having discarded the beaten silver breast decorations and Chwang clothing that they had once worn and adopted the loose, black trousers and shirt of Han peasant men.

The Chwang peoples, also known as the T'ai, have traveled a long road into eclipse since the time of Christ, when they ruled an empire that covered most of present-day China south of the Yangtze. Over the centuries most have been surrounded and assimilated by the dominant Han, or driven southward. The last great T'ai outbreak came in the eleventh century, when they were still strong enough under the chief Nung Chih-kao to lay siege to the city of Canton, although in the end they failed to take it. Other T'ai peoples migrated to Vietnam and Thailand, and to this latter country they gave a version of their name.

A mixture of Chwang weaknesses and Chinese strengths gave rise to this long retreat. Although initially occupying an enormous expanse of territory, the Chwang were weakened by their division into a large number of tribes and their failure to produce great leaders. The Chinese, with their unified political system, could from the beginning bring overwhelming military strength to bear on Chwang areas adjacent to areas they already ruled, gradually expanding their empire at the expense of the Chwang.

More important still to the Chinese advance was a highly sophisticated agriculture, until modern times the most advanced in the world, which they successfully applied to wet-rice cultivation in central and South China. There was an irony in this, for the typical grain crops of their ancient North China homeland were wheat and millet, and it was from the T'ai peoples that the Han learned to cultivate rice. But once familiar with this new crop, the industrious northern invaders excelled in producing it. In place of the wooden plows of the Chwang, they used plows of iron; rather than inefficiently casting the rice seed, they raised seedlings in a bed and transplanted them; instead of relying on rainfall, they built complicated irrigation systems; rather than trusting to the natural fertility of the earth, they built compost pits for human and animal waste and applied fertilizer to the fields. The result of these advances was that, where the Chwang had planted and harvested one rice crop a year, the Han realized two. The story of Cultivating Virtue Commune, where I had stopped the day before to talk with road laborers, had been repeated countless times throughout South China. It took arriving Chinese settlers only a generation or two to displace and assimilate the native Chwang population, "marrying their women and driving off their men." These were not victories of men and arms, but of agricultural expertise and hard work.

It was above all Chinese culture and civilization that formed the true cutting edge of Chinese imperialism. The Han Chinese possessed a written script, a highly developed Confucian philosophy, a long and rich recorded history, and an emperor who was said to be the son of Heaven. The Chwang could boast none of these things. Moreover, the Han were great propagandists, ceaselessly extolling the superiority of their own way of life while contemptuously dismissing the "uncouth" customs and folkways of the Chwang and other "southern barbarians" (*Nan-man*). Out of the real accomplishments of Chinese civilization there grew up over time a myth of Chinese cultural superiority, which worked its effect among the wealthier and more ambitious Chwang families of the border regions. Those who would otherwise have led their people in resistance—the great leaders—or who would have developed their own advanced systems of thought and agriculture—the great teachers—went over to the high-status Han culture, adopting Chinese surnames and customs. Within a generation these families would be denying their own heritage, claiming instead that their ancestors were Han Chinese from the north, and fabricating forged genealogies as evidence. As ordinary Chwang followed the lead of their elite, the Chinese cultural area would expand yet again.

Despite the numbers and historical importance of the Chwang, little is known about their customs. They left no written records of their own, and no systematic ethnographic study has ever been done. Chinese commentaries over the centuries make frequent mention of the group, but tend to focus on the same half-a-dozen attributes that from the standpoint of Confucian ideology seemed especially barbaric and worthy of contempt. Reports from Western missionaries were written from a different perspective but suffer from the same failing. Still, scattered, incomplete, and biased though the reports are, they provide some fascinating glimpses into the Chwang way of life.

The Chwang put enormous stock in their cattle and water buffaloes. Where the Chinese called a man rich who owned many fields, the Chwang counted his cattle and buffaloes. These animals were the currency of their land, and it was in heads of livestock that people calculated the price of a bride, a square of land, or a piece of silver jewelry. The central ritual of the spring planting festival involved the sacrifice of a live bull or cow, for nothing less would satisfy the Chwang gods.

These spring fertility rites seem also to have been the occasion for dancing, singing, and a fair amount of casual sex. These activities shocked the more reserved, even prudish, Chinese, who described them in very negative terms, and positively horrified Western missionaries, who were unable to bring themselves to describe them at all. One missionary account suggests the extreme sexual openness of the Miao, whom in this respect the Chwang resembled, more by what it doesn't say than by what it does. ". . . there are no decent women among the Miao, or there were none until the missionaries went among them. The Miao [of some districts] are so bad that they could hardly be worse. This is describing their moral condition in very few words, but these are quite enough. The less said on this topic the better. . . ."[2] Young Chwang women were expected to have relations with several men before marriage. Not only was chastity not valued, but some Chinese writers suggest that it was feared. To deflower a virgin was to risk pollution, and a girl's first lover could not marry her for fear that he would come to harm. Only after the birth of her first child, having proved her fertility, did a free-spirited woman settle down into wedlock. Because it was difficult to know who the father of the first child was, in Chwang society it was the second child, not the first, who enjoyed precedence.

The Chwang women were also said to be experts in the preparation and use of *ku,* a slow-acting but very lethal poison greatly feared throughout South China. To make *ku* they first caught several kinds of poisonous animals, including scorpions, snakes, centipedes, and geckos. These were placed together in a jar and, as they were not fed, before long they began to eat each other. When the last surviving animal, whose body contains the poisons of the others, is dead, it is dried and ground up. The resulting powder was the *ku.* It was often used on unfaithful male lovers, who could be given the antidote and saved if they returned and begged forgiveness in time.

As if this weren't enough, a form of oriental voodoo using doll images was also practiced. No wonder fearful Chwang men said of their women that they used sorcery to change into tigresses and devour men.

I would have preferred to spend a week in one of the Chwang hamlets we were passing. Then there would have been time to ask if women still prepared the *ku,* or if men still reckoned wealth in cattle. By the end of my visit, I would have gained an idea of how traditional Chwang culture was faring in its age-long struggle against Great Han chauvinism, the latest intrusions of which included such things as Marxist-Leninist-Maoist Thought and the agricultural commune. Such

---

[2] Samuel Clarke, *Among the Tribes in South-West China* (London: Morgan and Scott, 1911), p. 35.

a stopover was out of the question, for it would have been a violation of China's stringent travel regulations for foreigners. Still, there were signs that some elements of Chwang culture had survived.

Once, rounding a bend, I observed an enormous figure of a bull standing in a field a quarter-mile away from the road. The horns must have risen twenty feet above the ground. It was a rudely built structure, constructed mostly of wood, like the flotsam sculptures of the San Francisco Bay tide flats, and hung with cloth bunting. Had the Chwang, who once sacrificed live bulls during the spring festival, now turned to wooden images? The bull lay too far from the road to explore, and for once there was no village in sight where I could make inquiries. But it appeared certain that the spring fertility rites had been celebrated that year.

There was sometimes more to this continuation of outward forms than met the eye, however, as I found out when I stopped to take a picture of an attractive young Chwang girl. She was wearing the distinctive high apron, tied around the waist and fastened at the neck to the blue blouse underneath by one of the large silver brooches that I had seen other women wearing. She also had a carrying pole, but no burden dangling from it, slung across her shoulders.

"Don't get too close," Ming cautioned as I disembarked from the van. "She might hit you with her carrying pole."

I took this for a particularly droll bit of Ming humor, but I stopped my advance when she really did begin to limber up with her carrying pole.

"This is a camera," I explained. "I would like to take a picture of you." She did not shift her wary stance. Ming came hustling over with a local youth, who began to talk to her in Chwang. She was "illiterate," he told me. Like most of the Chwang women, she had never been to school, and could not speak Chinese.

"Tell her that her brooch is pretty," I said. This turned out to be the wrong thing to say. She clasped her hand to her brooch in alarm and then took an even more determined grip on her carrying pole. "She thinks you want her brooch," my translator told me. After a few more exchanges, the level of mutual understanding increased to the point where I could safely aim and shoot my camera, but at no time would she allow me to get near enough to get a close-up of her brooch.

Ming found all of this rather excessively amusing. After he had chortled "she thought that you were going to steal her brooch" three times, I asked him what was so funny. "You see," he replied, her brooch wasn't valuable at all. It was nothing more than worthless pot metal."

As he told it, in 1962 the People's Republic of China was in desperate straits. The Great Leap Forward had failed, leaving famine in its wake. The Soviet Union had withdrawn its technicians and had called in its loans, demanding immediate payment. The Chinese government was hungry for revenue, and dreamed up the movement it called with typical glibness "exchanging dead treasures for living treasures." The basic idea was that everyone in China would give up any valuables ("dead treasures") that they had in their possession—coins, gold, silver, paintings—to the government, which would in return issue commendatory certificates ("living treasures") to these "patriotic contributors." In the Chwang areas, the scheme had had to be modified somewhat. Since most of the Chwang did not speak or read Chinese and were unfavorably disposed toward their Han rulers, appeals to patriotism and paper certificates would not do. Instead, the Chwang women were told that in exchange for their silver brooches, bracelets, and rings, they would receive jewelry made of a newly discovered and quite valuable precious metal. What in fact they were given were brooches, bracelets, and rings made of aluminum or pot metal, neither of which metals the Chwang had ever seen before. Since the traditional brooches were large, weighing two or three ounces each, and since nearly every woman and girl wore one, the state must have collected millions of ounces of silver from the Chwang alone. It sounded like a sucker scheme invented by a traveling salesman, but it was perpetrated by the government of China on an unwitting minority. What amused Ming was not just the idea that an ignorant mountain maiden would think that a rich foreigner would bother stealing her worthless brooch, but that the real brooch had actually been stolen from her by the state two decades ago.

Over the course of the next several miles the road picked up a stream of foot traffic, indicating a rural market ahead. Most of the people we saw—and all of those who carried burdens of one kind or another—were women. Laden with two heavy baskets of vegetables, or with a giant bird's nest of branches balanced on their backs, they strode along with

swift and sure steps. One of the things that the Chinese had found un-
civilized about the Chwang was the way the men idled at home, while
the women worked in the fields and did the marketing. As one Chinese
writer in the eighteenth century, implicitly critical of what was to him an
improper reversal of roles, said, "The married women have a dark skin,
are well-fed, rarely sick, and very strong. In general, the women walk
around with their merchandise on their backs in the markets inside and
outside the cities, always trying to make a sale. . . . The men of these
women only play and they carry their children around with them the
whole day. When they have no children, they put their hands into their
sleeves and do nothing."[3] I couldn't speak for the behavior of the men,
but the women didn't seem to have changed much.

The market itself was located in a small and unimpressive commune
headquarters. Had it not been a market day, I am sure that we would
have driven through without stopping. We would have seen nothing of
interest. The entire commune seat consisted of a hundred yards of one-
story, whitewashed brick buildings, so flatly abreast along the narrow,
unpaved road that they had the feel of a Hollywood stage set.

But today was market day, the one day in five when the inhabitants
of a score or more hamlets within a day's walk, plus dozens of wandering artisans and peddlers, collected along this short stretch of street to
buy and sell, barter and trade. The press of the crowd forced us to a
crawl, and then stopped our forward progress entirely. All of a sudden,
an erect little man wearing a Red Army cap and flourishing the tiny red
flag of public security appeared at the driver's side of the van. He was so
short that his head barely topped the window. But he held his flag high,
and when he spoke it was to bark arrogantly at Ming: "Be careful when
you drive. There are a lot of people in town today." Since at that very
moment we sat becalmed in the very sea of humanity that he referred to,
these were things that Ming hardly needed to be told, and certainly not
in the tone of voice that the man used. Perhaps his failure to order the
masses had made him crotchety, or perhaps—because of his size—he
simply possessed in greater measure than most the officiousness that is
the mark of the Chinese petty official, but he acted like a little martinet.

[3] Cited in Wolfram Eberhard, *China's Minorities: Yesterday and Today* (Belmont, Calif.:
Wadsworth Publishing Company, 1982), p. 102.

Without waiting for Ming to reply he pranced off, shouting at the local Chwang and Han villagers in the same tone of voice that he had used on Ming.

As chaotic as the buying and selling occurring all around us appeared at first glance, the martinet and others of his ilk had gone to considerable trouble to impress order on it. There were submarkets given over to the sale of particular goods. Sellers sat within their ordained areas; only the buyers wandered freely about. Here the woodcutters sat on their haunches, their huge burden of branches on the ground beside them; there the sellers of pork stood behind a brace of bloody tables splayed with hunks of fatty meat. Behind them, in the open shed that served as abattoir, government butchers laid open porkers from snout to tail, carving them into two mirror-image perfect sides, one going to the villager who had raised the porker and the other to the state. Further on, the street was given over to the cackle of chickens, the quacking of ducks, and the honking of geese, and then to long rows of wicker baskets containing several kinds of garden vegetables, and finally to herbal medicines, their twisted roots and shriveled leaves giving no hint to the untrained of the potencies locked within.

But the most exciting area for me was the plaza of the artisans and foodsellers. For some time I wandered happily about this thirty-yard square. For a few minutes I watched a seal carver whittle the end of a matchbox-size piece of wood into the three characters of the waiting customer's name, for the Chinese still use seals and wax rather than signatures. Then I stood in front of the tiny stand of a wandering radio repairman, who to judge from his frayed and faded PLA jacket had learned his trade in the army, and saw him repair an old and battered radio; I wondered from what local peak you could pull in a signal. I examined the wares of an artisan who, using the bamboo and its leaves, could make everything from a woven fan to a peaked hat whose top was a perfect cone. I watched an old woman slurp down a bowl of gritty-looking cornmeal mush under the canopy of a flyblown food stall until my presence brought a scowl to her face. I wandered by a craftsman carving wooden bulls as small as the palm of his hand, miniature replicas of the giant symbol of spring and fertility that I had seen by the road earlier in the day, and saw him slap away the hand of a toddler who had grown too interested in his wares.

It was a market such as you would find in the countryside of any underdeveloped country, but with one difference. No artisans cried out their wares, no would-be buyers bargained hotly for a better price. Transactions tended to be carried out in a surreptitious, almost furtive manner. When I bought a handful of fried flour curls (ignoring Ming's warning against eating anything), my money disappeared instantly into the peddler's pockets as soon as I handed it to him, and he waved me off when I attempted conversation. Talk was so subdued that it blended in with the background noise, a low hum of conversation. It was like watching a movie of a rural market in which the sound had been turned down just low enough so that you couldn't make out the words. It didn't take me long to understand why. Standing over in front of an office building with a large red star stood an official. His hands were clasped behind his back and his expression was stern, as if not quite approving of all of this spontaneous mercantile activity. I spotted one or two other officials circulating in the plaza proper. Teng's order to reopen free peasant markets like this one had not met with the approval of all local officials, who saw the change as diminishing their control, and they still kept a careful watch. Woe be to the peasant or artisan who advertised his wares too loudly, or who bargained a little too hard. Teng may have said that it was all right to take the capitalist road, but the local guardians of Communist morality did not always agree.

Even if this temporary concentration of commercial activity was tolerated, more permanent manifestations were not. I asked a bearded old man, who with his traditional long gown and walking stick looked like a Chinese Rip Van Winkle, about local shops. He was reluctant to talk to me, and excused himself as soon as a crowd began to gather around us, but I did find out that the street had once been lined with shops, and that he had been the owner of one of them. There had been a winehouse, two teahouses, two noodle shops, a cake shop, two rice shops, a bambooware shop, an ironware shop, a furniture shop, a cloth shop, a medicine shop, a shoe shop, a shop selling coffins, and a shop selling incense, candles, and paper money for the departed ancestors. Now, he told me, we have one teahouse, one noodle shop, and one state sales store, all run by the government.

Because it was the only two-story building along that narrow street, the state sales store looked larger than it really was, which was about the size of a five-and-dime in an American small town. Crammed in its display cases and along its walls were hundred of goods, from cast-iron woks to plastic sandals, to basic items like needles, thread, salt, and vinegar. For the rest, the building was chockablock with people. It was, if anything, more crowded than the street, mostly with Chwang men and women who milled slowly about, taking in the wares. The clothes and ironware seemed to hold a particular fascination, for around these counters the crowd was frozen into a solid, motionless mass. But for all of the people in the store there was very little business being transacted. Occasionally someone did make a small purchase, a packet of thread or an ounce of salt, but most of those present, like tourists on a sightseeing tour, just gawked. A clerk, largely idle despite the crush, confirmed that the Chwang rarely bought anything. Their best customers, he said, were the officials and workers from the market town itself who had the money to buy the ready-made T-shirts, plastic ponchos, and thermos bottles that they sold. In effect, the store was run by the Chinese state for its own employees, who alone in the commune were a part of the cash economy. For the majority of the peasants, who expended their meager market earnings on necessities like salt, the store was part of the holiday entertainment of market day, a place to visit but not to shop.

There was one area of the store, however, where the Chwang crowded around with more purpose. It took me a minute to shoulder my way close enough to catch a glimpse of what it was they were willing to part with their meager cash to buy. I found myself facing a display of cast aluminum brooches and bracelets, including a box full of winged ornaments like the one that the young girl had been so ready to defend. Where native artisans had once worked silver into the intricate shapes demanded by Chwang custom, now the state cast aluminum trinkets to sell to the natives. If the villagers had been able to afford to buy more goods, the state sales store would have reminded me of a reservation trading post of the Great Han Father.

We went on, climbing into an ever more inhospitable landscape, and one that was home to mostly Chwang. The few poor huts scattered across each slope barely constituted the hardy collection of souls conjured up by the designation "hamlet." Although their dwellings were poorer and more primitive than those of the Chinese we had seen earlier, the aborigines paradoxically seemed the better dressed, especially the women in their blue aprons, white scarfs, and occasional elaborate headdresses, as if their diminishing resources had forced them to draw their aspirations even closer, to transer them from hut to person.

It was to such places that the Chwang had been displaced by the encroaching Chinese. The struggle between the Chinese and the Chwang had taken centuries, and it had resulted in the loss of the fertile lowlands of Kwangsi and in the Chwang's retreat to the rugged, poor, but defensible perimeter. Despite an official commitment to land reform, this historical expropriation went unredressed by the Chinese state. Rather, the opposite occurred. In 1958 the Chinese bureaucracy imposed restrictions on internal migration. The Chwang's one-time redoubts suddenly became reservations, which they were forbidden to leave. It must have looked to them like another, and even more pernicious, manifestation of Han imperialism.

On the surface, the minority policy of the PRC is an enlightened one. It is full of laudable declarations like "regional autonomy is practiced where the minority nationalities live in compact communities. . . . United, the people of all nationalities govern state affairs together."[4] But it is a sham.

Take the way "regional autonomy," for instance, is practiced in the Kwangsi Chwang Autonomous Region. Although most of China's twelve million Chwang reside within this region, established in 1958 largely following Kwangsi provincial boundaries, so do approximately twenty-five million Chinese, with the ironic result that even within their own "autonomous region" the Chwang remain a minority. This is also true of other ethnic groups, the borders of whose "autonomous" areas large and small are gerrymandered so that Chinese, and not the ethnic group in question, are in the majority. Submerging each minority in a sea of Chinese is one way to inhibit the development of an ethnic consciousness, while speeding assimilation to Han Chinese culture.

In Kwangsi, the Han domination starts at the top of the regional government—figureheads aside—and extends down to the production team, the lowest level of agricultural organization. Even when we visited entire settlements of Chwang, who were so little sinicized that

---

[4] *China: A Geographical Sketch* (Peking: Foreign Languages Press, 1974), p. 7.

men as well as women wore traditional clothing and few could speak Chinese, the leaders of the commune, the brigade, and the team were mostly Han men, often former members of the PLA who were assigned here after the completion of their term of military service. The right to self-determination of the Chwang homeland seemed to stop at the threshold of each Chwang family's hut. Above that modest level, the Chinese were everywhere firmly in charge.

The millennia-long struggle between the Chinese and the Chwang was nearing its long-delayed but inevitable end: the total absorption of the race that had once ruled all of South China. I knew they were a doomed people as I spoke with the young man who had helped me convince the Chwang girl with the brooch to let me take her picture. He was a bright, personable young man who spoke Mandarin without a trace of an accent. I asked him whether he himself was Chinese or Chwang.

"I am Han Chinese," he replied.

"And so do you speak Cantonese at home, or Mardarin?"

"Neither," he said, looking not the least bit discomfited. "At home we speak Chwang."

After the stolid timelessness of the hill villages we had passed through, it felt good to be back in the hopeful bustle of the county town of Nandan. The Chwang had seemed apathetic and lost; here the people were energetic and full of talk. The town, a crosswork of streets occupying an opening in the mountains, was shrunken by the altitude to the size of a Delta market town, but my spirits were lifted by the purposefulness of the residents as they walked or cycled home from work, and by the energy of the townsman who gave us directions to the only restaurant. It was probably because they ate better, I reflected.

The Nandan Restaurant was an ancient, two-story, wood-frame building that actually housed not one, but two, eateries. The ground floor was given over to the Chinese equivalent of a fast food restaurant: It sold bowls of hot noodles topped with chili sauce or sesame oil. Ming and I had survived the day on soda pop and dry crackers, and wanted something more substantial. We were directed up a steep flight of wooden stairs that creaked in protest under our combined weight, opening finally into a small restaurant. We took our seats happily, anticipating some mountain delicacy. ("They catch a lot of moles in the mountains," Ming had told me, smacking his lips.) The waitress came over.

"What's on the menu today?" Ming and I both spoke at once.

"Steamed rice and stir-fried greens."

"What else?"

"That's it."

We must have looked disheartened, for the waitress did not walk away but stood looking down at us. "If you want something else," she said, "they sell canned meat at the Tobacco and Cigarette Company [a state monopoly] across the road." She pointed at a neighboring table where two PLA officers in uniform sat dipping their chopsticks alternately into their rice bowl and a can of duck meat with its lid twisted up out of the way. "We have a can opener," the waitress ended helpfully.

"This would never happen in the Delta," Ming said with a grin that managed to convey both superiority and incredulity, after the waitress had left. We decided we needed something besides rice and greens, and Ming went out to purchase a can of meat and a tin of cookies.

I looked around the restaurant. Though it was dinnertime, only three of the eight tables were occupied. At one table an older man and young woman sat eating quietly. Dressed in slacks, a silken-looking shirt, and a pair of highly polished shoes, the man was unusually well-attired for this backwoods outpost, and I figured him for an army officer also, higher-ranking than the two in uniform. There was probably a base nearby. Most minority areas had Red Army encampments in the vicinity to forestall the possibility of an uprising.

From a table at the other end of the room came a sound that often accompanies meals in China—the noisy staccato of rowdy young workers playing the "finger game." In its simplest variation this is the "rock, scissors, and paper" game that American children sometimes play (which may itself be Chinese in origin). Here the four youths were engaged in "beating the tiger," a version that is only slightly more elaborate than the "scissors game," but infinitely more clamorous. The two players begin by each holding out a chopstick in their right hands, crossing them as if they were about to engage in a swordfight. Keeping time by beating the chopsticks together, they slowly chant in rising crescendo: "Two . . . brothers . . . are . . . we. . . ." When they reach this point, they bring the chopsticks together one final time with some force (bamboo chopsticks have been known to break at this point) and shout "club" or "tiger" or "chicken" or 'insect." The climax of the game has been reached, and the winner is decided as follows: The club beats the tiger but is helpless against the insect (which is presumably a termite); the chicken loses to the tiger but wins out against the insect. In cases where both players shout out the same name, or where they shout out "chicken" and "club," or "insect" and "lion," it is a standoff. The game continues until one of the fatal relationships mentioned above is reached. Each time this happens, the loser has to down a drink to the good-natured jeers of his fellows. It is a pleasant, convivial game, like dice in a barroom, except that it is a game of skill as much as of chance. The fall of the dice may be random, but human beings are not. A player who allows himself to fall into a pattern recognized by his opponent can scarcely expect to go home sober.

On the far side of the room from the workers, standing in the corner behind the stairwell, so quietly that I missed them on my first sweep of the room, were the children. There were three in all, an achingly thin girl of ten or so, a tiny infant of only a few months who was strapped to the girl's back by means of a piece of cloth cross-tied about her chest, and a grubby toddler of about three, who stood close by the girl's side. As soon as the young workers made signs of getting up to leave, the girl rushed over to their table, toddler in tow. She picked up a pair of chopsticks and began finishing off the leftovers, a few scraps of vegetables and grains of rice, popping the food alternately into her own and her two charges' mouths. Each time the beak-like chopsticks neared them, the younger children's mouths gaped open automatically, like those of nestlings. When there were no more scraps to be gleaned, the older girl picked up one of the bowls and began to lick it clean, an action clumsily aped by the toddler. Within a minute the insides of all the bowls glistened wetly with spittle, and there was not a scrap of food in sight.

The reason for their speed and furtiveness soon materialized in the person of the waitress, who came bustling out of the kitchen chiding them for "stealing food." Though she chased them partway down the stairs, she did it in the half-hearted, kindly manner of someone guiltily shooing off a stray cat, not wanting to feed it for fear it will stay. The children sensed this, running only as far as the bottom of the stairs. As soon as she turned her back, they creeped stealthily back up to the top of the stairs and resumed their vigil, their little heads poking alertly out of the stairwell. When the two uniformed officers got up to leave, the earlier scene was repeated: the dash to the table, the short work with the chopsticks and then with the tongue, and finally the climactic appearance of the waitress. It was so well choreographed, like scenes from a melodrama, that I suspected the waitress of being in secret league with the ragged children, giving chase only after she was sure that they had finished the meager table scraps. Too afraid to feed the children because it was against regulations, she was at the same time too compassionate to drive them off until they had eaten a little something.

The next time the waitress disappeared into the kitchen, I called the girl over. She came over, but warily stood just out of reach like a half-wild animal. She had nothing of the big-city bravado of the gamins we had met in Liuchow, and she answered my questions with silence. Perhaps she did not understand Mardarin, but Ming's awkward-sounding attempts to communicate in Chwang fared no better. She understood what a cookie in an outstretched hand meant, though, instantly relieving me of it and stuffing it into her mouth. Her eyes narrowed with concentration as she quickly chomped and swallowed. I gave her a second cookie and this time it went to the three-foot-high toddler, who I guessed was her younger brother. He took only a second longer than his sister to devour it. Curious now to see what she would do with a third cookie, I held it out. This time it was deposited in a pocket, saved to crumble into the baby's mouth later, I was sure. She took as good care of her little brood as she could under the circumstances. I decided that we could do without cookies, and gave the entire box to her. Her eyes widened at this unexpected gift, and she scuttled off down the stairs without a word, perhaps frightened that I would change my mind, or that someone else would relieve her of this treasure. Or maybe to share it with the rest of her hungry family. Such self-sacrifice was expected of elder daughters in Chinese families.

''How was the meal?'' a voice asked in Cantonese. It was the waitress, who told me that she had overheard us speaking her native dialect. She announced that she herself was from Chan-chiang, a coastal city in southern Kwangtung. There, shortly after the Liberation, she had met and married her husband, at that time a noncommissioned officer in the

PLA. Then, shortly afterwards he had mustered out, and had unexpectedly been transferred to Nandan. That had happened twenty-eight years ago, and she had not seen home or family since. No wonder she reacted to us as if we were childhood friends. She had been exiled in this remote mountain town for nearly three decades.

I asked her about the urchins.

"This is a poor county," she said, "not like Kwangtung. The peasants in the communes around the town get between four and five hundred catties of rice, corn, and sweet potatoes a year, and have almost no cash income. They are very poor, and some of them send their children into town to beg. We have at least a dozen children come to the restaurant every day. Like the ones you saw."

"Where do they sleep?"

"The boys sleep wherever they can to get out of the weather. The girls are mostly from the closer villages and go home every night."

"What is it like back in the mountains?" I voiced a question that had been troubling me. "Away from the main road."

"I don't know. I've never been there." She hesitated a little, and then brought the conversation back around to her own plight. "Even we government employees in the town cannot collect enough grain from the peasants to have pure rice at every meal, so we mix in corn. At home in Kwangtung we used to feed corn and sweet potatoes to the pigs."

I had been surprised to find kernels of corn mixed in with my rice, but had eaten the mixture anyway. Ming had not, rather eating his rice around them, as you eat around a wormy spot in an apple. In the bottom of his otherwise-clean rice bowl he had left a small pile of golden kernels. I showed it to her.

"That's nothing," she said to her fellow provincial. "Here in the restaurant we mix in nine parts rice to one part corn. At home we have to mix in two parts rice to one part corn to make our ration last to the end of the month." Ming groaned in sympathy.

The waitress had given us directions to the local county reception center, but had seemed doubtful that we would be able to find lodgings there. And so it was. "No vacancy," a bored-looking clerk told us at the reception center office. One glance at the makeup of the crowd that our arrival had drawn out of the rooms told us why. It was not a crowd of male cadres traveling on official business but of women and children, entire family groups. I did not need Ming to figure out what had happened. The state had disbursed funds to build a reception center like the one we had stayed in at Te-ch'ing. But after the center had been completed, county officials had quietly divided it up among kith and kin. We were sent on our way with directions to the county hostel.

The hostel was little more than a dormitory for truckers. Its rooms contained nothing but a tier of bunkbeds along each wall and a small stand with a thermos. The pit toilets and bath stalls were out back. But at eighty fen a night it was hard to find fault. After all, I had paid twenty times that the night before in Liuchow. Besides, I would rather stay at a truck stop with Chinese than be pampered, isolated, and extorted at a hotel for foreigners. It was better for understanding to rough it with the truckers.

But I had reckoned without one of the most attractive characteristics of the Chinese, their innate courtesy toward strangers. No sooner had I sat on my bunkbed to examine the two threadbare and greying cotton pads that served as cover and mattress than the young attendant who had led us to our room appeared with an armful of bedding. She swept the musty cotton pads off the bed and replaced them with the clean bedding she had brought, a mattress and a thick cotton comforter with colorful designs. She disappeared without a word, only to reappear a minute later with an extra thermos bottle of hot water and a pair of what looked like Japanese getas, sandals with a square wooden sole and cloth thongs.

''Wear these when you go to take your bath,'' she said as she disappeared for the second time. ''And call me if you need anything.''

''Foreign guest,'' Ming sneered amiably at me after she was gone, looking ruefully at the thin cotton pads on his own bunk. It was only after I traded him the heavy mattress in return for one of his pads that he was slightly mollified.

I suppose that my clacking down the hall (I have never learned to wear getas properly) alerted the attendant that I had emerged for my bath, for she had a bucket of hot water ready for me when I arrived out back. She also insisted on carrying this heavy wooden bucket out to the wash stall, even though she was a head shorter and probably sixty pounds lighter than I. We walked along to the mixed stares—amused and curious—of a half-a-dozen truckers, who of course had fetched their own water.

She sat the bucket of water down in the stall and straightened up. "Be careful that you don't slip," she admonished loudly. "And call me if you need more water."

Not on your life, I thought as I latched the wooden door shut. So sparingly did I wash myself down that I still had a third of a bucket left when I finished.

The evening cooled off rapidly, and the heavy cotton comforter proved necessary. There was something in the damp evening chill that signaled the remoteness of this town, with its single dirt road linking it to the outside world. I felt as though I were in the back of beyond, a Chinese Timbuktu which few visited and even fewer escaped. Certainly the waitress had regarded her nearly thirty years here as a form of banishment, and had never stopped longing for the tropical humors of her home by the South China sea. But her husband had a good position in the county administration, and she a much-prized job in a restaurant, making them better off than all but a few of Nandan county's half-million inhabitants. For all its lack of roads, the county was not a trackless waste—there were few places in China where the tramp of feet had not worn paths—but it was a high mountain fastness, its rugged terrain holding its inhabitants in thrall. It was somehow appropriate that the town sat astride the only road out of this wilderness, for the most important responsibilty of this bastion of party control was to make sure that the peasants stayed put.

CHAPTER SIX

The Hungry Earth

W E left Nandan in a cold morning drizzle that cast a grey pall like an inverted bowl over the valley. It was half past seven. The road was a pandemonium of cadres and workers on their way to work. They sat high and erect on their bicycles, the expert cyclists of China, one hand deftly guiding their forward motion, the other primly holding a black umbrella perfectly erect above them. Down in the fields that stretched off to either side of the road, the peasants were already at work, standing ankle-deep in paddy mud, their conical bamboo hats offering scant protection from the wet. To see the contrast between the mud-slogging peasants below and the peddling workers and cadres above was to begin to understand the enormous divide between these two groups. It is not just that workers and officials are free of the tyranny of the seasons, the weather, and the earth, while peasants are still in thrall. This much is true of farmers and factory workers in all Third World countries. What widens class differences in China beyond all reason is that a baby's future occupation is fixed at birth, inherited from its parents, so that workers beget only workers, peasants beget only peasants.

We had left the town behind, and all of rural China's blameless savagery reasserted itself. A gaggle of peasant women on the roadway, pants rolled up and ankles black with mud; another group bent over in the fields. A boy leading a gently ambling water buffalo, the lower body of the beast caked with great cracking scabs of mud; another buffalo moving at the same effortless pace, even though sunk to its knees in a sea of clinging mud and harnessed to a wooden plow.

Then the fields were behind us and we were climbing a steep slope out of the Nandan Valley, tires occasionally spinning in dirt loosened by the rain. We were back in the mountains.

"*Yang chang xiao lu,*" I heard Ming mutter under his breath. "Goat intestine road" was what the Chinese called a narrow, twisting, turning road. The name fit. The road went every which way but straight, going up and down, left and right, in endless, dizzying succession. Several times we came to places that seemed impassable, but the road, with serpent-like cunning, always triumphed eventually.

The rain stopped shortly after 9:00 A.M., and I became anxious to call a halt, as much for a respite from the road's intestinal meanderings as to plot another point on the graph of rural poverty. Settlements were scarce in this wilderness, however, and it was fifteen minutes before we hit a level stretch and I spotted paddy fields and huts.

Ming stopped dead in the center of the road.

"Don't you want to pull over to the shoulder?" I asked.

"What for?"

What for indeed. We were on the main road (there was a second road far to the west, I saw from my map) connecting the provinces of Kwangsi and Kweichow, each as big and as populated as Spain, but we hadn't seen a single vehicle since leaving Nandan. The other truckers had headed back east. Even the bicycles had vanished a few minutes outside that town. With the exception of ambling villagers and a water buffalo or two, the road had been ours this morning.

Rice transplanting was under way in the nearest field, where stooped-over peasants formed a ragged line of advance. The field beyond was being harrowed: A water buffalo mushed along at its customary hypnotic pace, pulling a long wooden board studded with small pegs. This smoothed the muddy earth and at the same time laid down a grid of lines for the transplanters to follow. Each of these cradled in his left arm a muddy block of sprouted seedlings. With his free hand he broke off a small piece containing half-a-dozen shoots and, holding it firmly between thumb and fingers, plunged the root end wrist-deep into the soft mud. The peasants worked with the speed of long practice. So quickly did they advance that it seemed slight of hand that left rows of tiny young plants standing erect where a moment before there had been only a sea of mud.

Ming had fallen into conversation with a buck-toothed fellow who spoke passable Mandarin. Like most of the hill peasants we spoke with on the road, this fellow was a local official, a team head, whose position freed him from field work and gave him the time and poise to talk to strangers. He was, like most officials, a born busybody, making everybody's business his own. He had a redoubtable array of data at his command, the product of years of reporting up the chain of command on everything from pigs ("ten, four more than last year") to people ("sixty-five total in the team divided into eleven families, comprising twenty-two able-bodied, twenty-eight children, and five elders"). His store of production figures went back twelve years, the length of time that he had held office, and he recited the figures with the singsong voice of a schoolboy reading a poem. But even this official savant became subdued when asked about bicycles (none), radios (none), tractors (none), and watches (one—his own).

The conversation left Ming less than his usual cheerful self. "Pretty bad, isn't it" he said simply, for once not gloating over the superiority of his province and his people.

The railroad from Liuchow to Kweiyang ran through the valley, straight and true on its raised bed. The guardrail—a simple wooden pole—was down as we came up to the crossing, and the crossing keeper, an old man in a faded PLA cap, was standing by. A superannuated Kwangsi guerrilla, it was his responsibility to make sure that the tracks were clear of peasants, water buffalo, and carts for the trains that came by a dozen times daily. Behind him stood a little brick cottage, smaller than the ramshackle huts we had just passed, but snugly and cleanly built, and fronted with a row of jasmine in bloom, the first flowers I had seen outside of the cities. A comfortable cabin, a flower garden, a modest salary, rice rations delivered to his door thrown from the speeding train—these were the rewards of serving the revolution that he listed for me. But this man, peasant-born, neglected to mention the greatest revolutionary boon of all: He had escaped peasanthood.

There was a larger moral to the crossing, which I realized as the locomotive, a big coal-burner pulling a dozen freight cars, came hurtling by full throttle. Trains didn't stop in this valley. They didn't even appear to slow down. They sought this level ground only because it was the easiest route between Liuchow and Kweiyang. Like all the PRC's trains, this one was bound from one city to another, and took no note of the smaller settlements along its course. In most Third World countries there is a train station in every village that the tracks pass, even if only the local trains stop. Not in China. In the country with the greatest number of villages of all, there are stations in the county seats, but rarely in anything smaller. In other underdeveloped countries the train is the most democratic of conveyances, the place for Central American peasants to catch a ten-cent ride to the local market town to sell a dollar's worth of spinach leaves. In China the train is a superurban transit system, used by workers, soldiers, and bureaucrats. The trains might as well run underground, or in the sky, for the possibility that a resident of this valley had of boarding one.

We moved on and the wilderness closed in again. Giant ravines cut the landscape into steep, heavily vegetated slopes, and only the occasional patchwork of corn and sweet potato fields, or a cluster of thatched huts, reminded us that here too peasants were somehow eking out a living. The road, which on previous days had occasionally forked, now simply went on and on without a break, as if it were all it could do to find its own way through these mountains. It was not just that we encountered no other main roads (which in China are so few that they can be shown on a map the size of an open book), but even the rutted tracks that before had signaled a nearby commune market town were absent. Still, at intervals, we caught sight of narrow paths worn by generations of peasant feet winding off into the mountains, and there was the occasional cluster of thatched huts, although now at some remove from the road.

This was Mao country. It was primarily on the strong backs and stoic endurance of peasants living in poor, mountainous regions like this one that the Communists had ridden to power. Indeed, not many miles south of the road, one of the earliest of the Communist base areas had been located. On December 11, 1929, the Right River Soviet had been established under the direction of Teng Hsiao-p'ing, who became its political chief. At its height, the Soviet controlled nine counties in northwestern Kwangsi, and its military force, the Red Seventh Army, numbered ten thousand strong. As they had with the rebels of previous dynasties, peasants here had cast their lot with the insurgents in large numbers. They had little to lose and, if the blandishments of Communist propagandists were to be believed, a world to gain. The Right River Soviet was soon crushed, though through no fault of its peasant supporters. In mid-1930, the Central Committee of the Chinese Communist Party ordered the Red Seventh Army into another province. Left virtually undefended, the Soviet was invaded almost immediately by forces of the provincial government, and many of its supporters were executed.[1]

There was a question that had never been answered: What had been done for this and other backward and destitute regions whose support had been critical to the Communist movement, after its success? What had been their fate after the promised land—the cities and rich lowland regions that comprise China proper—had been won? I had never before left the road, but now I had to visit those tiny huts. Ming chose to stay in the van. I suspected that he had seen enough.

I stepped off the road and was at once engulfed by heavy vegetation. I could no longer see the van. Even the path I had thought to follow was overgrown, and the underbrush pulled and clung as I passed. It was no longer raining, but the grey, indistinct mass of the low-hanging clouds gave the setting a sodden dreariness. The rain had stilled the insects and birds, and I could hear nothing except the sound of my own passage. When I hesitated, the world became preternaturally quiet. The absence of any wildlife in the midst of such luxuriant greenery was disconcerting, making it seem a counterfeit Eden. Still, I had hardly expected to come upon deer or giant pandas. The animals that had once abounded in these hills had over the centuries been conquered by man. They had been killed for food and for skins.

It was as I topped the first knoll that I began to hear it, a faint percussion in the distance. I crossed down into a small ravine, the steep path slippery where the sun had not been able to find it. Steppingstones had been placed at the bottom, and water stood in small, marshy pools. In a

---

[1] Diana Lary, *Region and Nation: The Kwangsi Clique in Chinese Politics, 1925–1937* (London: Cambridge University Press, 1974), pp. 102–108.

hard rain, this way would be impassable. The sound had grown into a rhythmic thudding by the time I reached the far side of the ravine, and appeared to be coming from the more heavily wooded slope in front of me. I stepped through the trees and sighted the source of the noise.

I was facing a small clearing, half surrounded by earthern huts. There, an old man of indeterminate age was pounding grain into flour, using a primitive device of ancient lineage, a pedal tilt hammer. A log sat on a fulcrum like a lopsided seesaw. The old man would step onto the short end, raising the hammer end high in the air, then he would take his weight off again, allowing gravity to bring it thudding down onto the pestle and mortar below. Each blow drove the tight-fitting pestle a fraction of an inch further down into the mortar. After hundreds or thousands of repetitions, the grain in the mortar would be reduced to a coarse flour. I later found that identical pedal tilt hammers had been excavated from Han dynasty tombs of the first century B.C., a full twenty-one hundred years ago. At the time, I knew only that I was looking through a crack in time's door back into an age where no electric motors hummed, no diesel engines stroked, and no machined gears ground grain effortlessly into a fine stuff, an age in which simple devices of wood and stone were all that stood between man and nature.

"Grandfather, have you eaten yet?" I hailed him, but he took no notice of me, continuing his lonely up-and-down dance. At first I thought that he was blind and deaf, for even when I approached to within a few feet and saluted him again he did not seem aware of my presence. What made me uncertain were his eyes, which were not closed or clouded over, but appeared to be looking straight ahead, rigidly and with fear. One of the ways that a Chinese fends off an evil ghost is by ignoring it, in this way preventing the ghost from gaining a foothold in his consciousness. I wondered if my appearance in this remote ravine was so foreign to the sum of this old man's existence that it seemed to him an unreal apparition, a ghost, and he could not respond for fear of losing his sanity, literally.

Close by the old man, sitting motionless on a flat stone bench, were two young boys. They may have been his grandsons, or equally likely, his great-grandsons, for there was no guessing the span of years that separated them. The boys were tiny creatures, with spindly legs and close-cropped heads too large for their bodies. Neither had clothes that fit. The one sat corseted in a jacket two sizes too small, while the sleeves of the other's oversized shirt hung down over his hands like a mandarin's robe. But what struck me most forcibly were the boys' dull, incurious eyes and their stillness. Taking their cue from their grandfather, they did not return my greeting.

Made of large, ill-formed mud bricks mixed with straw, and covered with a ragged thatch, the huts would scarcely have made respectable cow pens in the Delta. (I had not seen any water buffaloes, nor did I expect to, for they would have been useless on these paddyless slopes.) They were homes that would compare unfavorably with a tar-paper shack in one of Rio's hillside slums. In Brazil and other Third World countries, even in the poorest, most wretched regions, the dwelling places offer a mute hope of a better life somewhere else. Sometimes it comes in the form of the flotsam that holds down the roofs—pieces of rusting car parts, worn tires. Other times it is to be seen in walls of hammered tin or cardboard, or in windows of salvaged glass and plastic. But always there is something. Here in these huts there was nothing manufactured, nothing connecting this village with the age of machines or of electronics.

I stepped inside the nearest doorway, and was met with a darkness broken only by a faint light from one small window cut high in the wall. I stood motionless for a second to allow my eyes to adjust to the gloom, and gradually the interior took shape. This was life pared down to its irreducible minimum.

What I saw was a cave of earth, the uneven earthern floor of a piece with the rough walls. Against the right wall was a stove, made of the same mud bricks that formed the walls and topped with a few squares of fire-hardened red tile. The fire was out now, but I could see next to the stove the large pile of dried grass and kindling that served as fuel, and on the stove the crude crockery pots used for cooking. The stove could not have been well ventilated, for the entire wall above was covered with a layer of carbon black. Facing the door on the far wall was a wooden board, hung from the adobe wall on two wooden pegs. On that shelf, covered with dust and cobwebs, there was an ancestral tablet, a simple wooden plaque, fronted by a small pottery cup filled with the charred stubs of homemade incense sticks. To the left, in the darkest corner of the hut, I could make out two wooden sleeping platforms, covered with woven bamboo mats. What looked like a mound of old rags was on the floor beside the platforms. Otherwise, the hut was bare. Ancestral tablet aside, there was not one thing in the hut not directly related to survival, to meeting the gut needs of shelter and food.

I was just turning to go when I caught a motion out of the corner of my eye. The bundle of rags rolled over, righted itself, and then began to crawl rapidly toward me. It came right up to my feet and stopped, and I saw that it was an infant. Only its hands, feet and head protruded from the grimy garments that I had mistaken for rags. Too young to recognize me for a stranger, it was utterly unafraid, its face regarding me with the openmouthed grin of infantile curiosity. I put the little one's age at about ten months. Its mother was undoubtedly at work on the sloping fields, and had left the baby on the floor to amuse itself, probably entrusted to the care of the elderly stoic outside. I spoke to it for a second and then turned to go.

The view out the door of the cave home was limited to the clearing, the low trees, and the ravine below. Here on this slope the world did not extend much further than the flickering light cast by a tribal campfire. Few were the activities that did not center around the never-ending task of staving off hunger. In the evening I could imagine the grandfather gathering his grandsons at his feet, and telling them tales of emperors and dragons, but only after the day's ration of corn was slowly pounded into meal. The mother would return home from the fields as dusk fell to prepare the evening meal of cornmeal mush, and with that vital task out of the way would have time to hold her child. On feast days, surely, everyone would eat a little better, and for that reason give thanks to their ancestors. But it seemed unlikely that their grandparents had been much worse off, or that their children would be much better off, than they were right now. The borders of their lives—their huts, their hillside plots—had long been fixed by natural forces beyond their control. The economic alchemy that can take such conditions and transmute them into wealth has not yet been invented.

I never found out the name of this hamlet, if it had a name, but I passed a hundred like it over the next fifty miles.

The mountains broke suddenly, and we came onto the high, wind-swept Yunkwei plateau. A winged obelisk stood on the left-hand side of the road, marking the boundary between Kwangsi and Kweichow provinces. The inscription leaped out at me as we approached: "The Twenty-third Year of the Republic (1934)." I could not have been more surprised if I had found a Nationalist Chinese flag flying. In a country in which all monuments and inscriptions referring to the Republic of China had been systematically obliterated, a country in which history had been rewritten (and was still being rewritten) around the exploits of the Communist Party, this stone obelisk still held its message that a republic (not a people's republic) had once ruled here. It must have been raised upon completion of the road and, through some bureaucratic oversight, still stood.

The current order was not content with mere border markers. Only a few hundred yards further on, we were flagged down (again the little red flag) by three men in blue Mao uniforms. They swarmed over the van, poking into our boxes and asking for papers. "What are you looking for?" I asked one of them, but neither he nor his comrades replied. They were a silent, unfriendly group. I was glad when we were waved on our way.

"They were from the Ministry of Transportation," Ming told me as soon as we had put a little distance between ourselves and the border. "They were searching for contraband goods. A lot of smuggling goes on in Kweichow. The quota of bicycles or leather shoes assigned here by the state never sells out. Too few of the locals can afford to buy them for their own use. So they buy them and turn around and sell them to outsiders like drivers. This is a poor province."[2]

Even the Chinese regard Kweichow as a hole. Originally its name was written with the character "Kwei" meaning "Devils," probably because of the presence of the Miao, a fierce collection of hill tribes who had not taken to Han colonization and had staged repeated uprisings throughout Chinese history, the last in the 1930s. There were many military bases in Kweichow, the "Region of the Devils," in traditional times for the purpose of restraining these unsubdued tribes. Later, when it became a province, the mandarins substituted the homophonic character "Kwei" meaning "precious" or "noble." It was a singularly in-

[2] In 1979 Kweichow had the lowest average collective income (46 yuan), and the lowest reported life expectancy (59 years), of any province. See Nicholas Lardy, *Agriculture in China's Modern Economic Development* (Cambridge: Cambridge University Press, 1983), p. 171.

appropriate choice. For Kweichow was anything but rich. It shivers in
the reputation of being one of the poorest, least fertile, and most insular
of all the Chinese provinces. It is an inland plateau, a high, inhospitable
island of bleakness in the otherwise lush hill-and-valley landscape of
South China. Ming, now warmed up on the subject, cited an ancient
folk rhyme. Probably intended to discourage people from immigrating
to this wasteland, it went:

> There are not three feet level
> in all of Kweichow,
> and no one has more than
> three taels of silver.

Kweichow had been conquered before the birth of Christ, but it had
remained an outpost of the empire long after other outposts had been
drawn into the settled sweep of Chinese soil. It was an area favored by
the emperor for banishment. Here the famous Ming dynasty philospher
Wang Yang Ming had been exiled for three years when he fell out of
court favor. At the time—the sixteenth century—he had described this
far end of the empire as wild and barbaric. It didn't seem to have
changed much.

Kweichow's nickname is "China's Switzerland," which gives a
good sense of its rugged, landlocked geography, but is completely
misleading as regards its charm. The countryside was desolate. It was
birdless, treeless, and bleak, entirely barren of the profusion of
undergrowth that had given to the Kwangsi mountainsides behind us
their (false) sense of profligacy. Paddy snaked its way about the lower
slopes of elevations like contour lines translated into bas-relief, but it
was a poor paddy, sparsely planted.

The seasons had changed with the elevation. In the Delta, summer
had come; here it was only spring. There the first rice crop had been
knee-high and looking to head into grain; here the first and only rice
crop had just been moved from the seed beds into the fields. In the Delta
the rice had been planted thickly, in bunches only a hand or two apart;
here in the paler plateau soil, the bunches had to be spaced a foot or
more apart so that they would not stunt one another. "Man feeds the
earth; the earth feeds man" (*ren yang ti, ti yang ren*), the Chinese say, but
the equation is not that simple. Lowland paddy feeds man willingly and

generously; the seedlings pushed up by the fertile mud grow like weeds where they are not wanted and yield a bountiful harvest. Here the fields were like ungrateful offspring, slow to repay the care and concern that had been so painstakingly lavished on them. This was land that even traditional Chinese agriculture, efficient though it was, could not make prosperous. It enabled the settlers to scrabble out a toehold, but not to enlarge it; to survive, but not to accumulate. However counterintuitive it may seem to Americans believing in the inevitability of progress, scrabbling for survival is where matters have stayed for the peasants of Kweichow generation after generation, for a thousand years.

The dwellings we were seeing were proof enough of that. Often constructed even more poorly than those on the mountainsides of Kwangsi had been, they were Stone Age huts. Their walls started with a foundation of rough stones, stacked to a height of three feet, no more. Given the crudeness of the stonework, the walls would have crumbled had they gone any higher. On top of this were usually six courses of mud brick, bringing the walls up to shoulder height. The space between the top of the walls and the roof was filled with woven mats tied to a wooden frame, and the roof itself was a thin layer of thatch over wattle. Occasionally, a rocky hill served as the back wall of a handful of huddled huts, crouching like a crude version of Hopi Indian cliff dwellings. They were minimal shelters against the blustering winds and chilling cold of a high-plateau winter, but they resisted the almost daily rains of the plateau better than an all-adobe hut would have.

The peasants were paying for the sins of some remote ancestor, who somehow saw in these hills the promise of a livelihood better than he had enjoyed at his place of birth. Maybe the siren that had led him into this wilderness was the prospect of having his own land. Maybe it was drought that drove him here, or famine that had made him look with favor on these hills. There was no definitive answer. But if it was a mystery why the forefathers had settled in such an ungrateful environment, it was perfectly clear why the descendants had stayed: Since 1958 it has been a crime to change your place of residence without official permission, a law primarily designed to staunch the flow of people from the countryside into the cities.

The road, which had been no more than a rutted track in the mountains, now unwound wide and smooth over the plateau. As if sensing my mood, Ming accelerated. It made no difference. The condition of this bleak country was apparent at a glance. We passed a peasant whose blues had been patched and repatched so many times that it was hard to tell where the patches left off and the original cloth began. It seemed pointless to inquire about his income. And it seemed certain that the diet of the inhabitants of these poor huts would fall well below the standards of United Nations nutritionists. It was only after passing through Tu-shan, "Solitary Mountain," that I saw something worth stopping for.

Ahead, on a small knoll, like a tableau of a medieval fair, was a horse market. Most markets are held in commune seats or larger towns, but a few, like this one, were held in out-of-the-way places where no houses are to be seen. The undersized cart ponies, whose heads reached only to my shoulder, stood unmoving, the only motion their manes ruffling in the wind. The men, carters I guessed, far outnumbered the ponies. A few were up examining horseflesh. Most were in the perpetual squat of the peasant, looking as stolid as their standing ponies. I grabbed my camera and walked up the knoll, shooting as I went.

As I was taking pictures, I asked a few of the squatting men how much the ponies were selling for. They looked away and did not reply. Maybe that was too sensitive a topic at a horse market. I decided to try another tack.

"How have things changed since the revolution?" I put the question to an avuncular-looking carter who I guessed was old enough to know. He looked away, but the cigarette I offered him went quickly into his pocket. Finally he answered, in a voice as rasping as the wind: "Now we have rubber tires on our carts."

Now we have rubber tires on our carts.

This, I thought, as I continued taking pictures, could stand as a metaphor of the accomplishments of the last thirty years. Sandals were made of plastic rather than woven straw, but peasants were still shod in sandals; tires made of rubber had replaced wooden cart wheels, but transportation was still limited to pony-drawn carts. Change outside of the cities had been incremental rather than revolutionary, gradual improvements in the fabric of a life still strikingly primitive.

As I was taking another picture I noticed a youngish man approaching and asked him the price of ponies, hoping that he would be less reticent than the others. But I didn't get the answer I was hoping for. Rather he said, more belligerently than I had yet heard any Chinese speak: "Do you have a permit to take pictures?"

During the course of a year in China I had never heard of such a thing, and told him so. I looked to take another picture.

"It is forbidden to take pictures here," he snarled, stepping aggressively up to me.

What could be illegal about taking pictures of this innocent scene, I thought. I stepped around him to get another shot of the market.

He loomed up in front of me again, this time much closer, and looking ominously at my camera.

Though he was wearing only a ragged olive-drab PLA jacket and pants, I suddenly noticed that he had on leather sandals, in sharp contrast to the plastic and straw sandals of the other men. I decided that he was probably an overzealous Communist cadre, of whom there are many in China, making sure that the peasant men paid taxes on their sales and purchases and keeping order in the market. I clicked the lens cover back on my camera and started back to the van.

He reached out and grabbed my arm. "Show me your papers or I will take you to the public security bureau."

With this bully on the prowl, I could understand why the men had been afraid to talk to me. I handed him my travel permit. He looked at it for a long time, but finally handed it back to me without a word. Turning on his heel, he walked away. As we drove off, I realized that he hadn't shown me any identification, nor said a word about his position. I had assumed that he was a state cadre because he acted like one. Cadres are omnipresent in China, and like the Chinese themselves I had learned to avoid confrontations. But the incident continued to trouble me as we drove on.

An hour later we dropped down slightly from the high plateau into the valley of the Tou River, the "Head River," whose waters eventually joined those of the Yangtze. The road became paved, people appeared in some numbers, and bikes and even an occasional Russian-style truck put in an appearance. Ahead I saw the city that was the source of this largesse, Tu-chun.

I wouldn't have stopped again if the city's park had not been adjacent to the main road. As it was, a walk in the park seemed just the thing I needed to stretch my legs, cramped after the long ride. But I had no sooner walked through the gate when I began to be followed by several Chinese youths. As I walked by the icestick stands, took pictures of couples (of the same sex) dancing to music from a small cassette recorder, and admired the cages of singing birds, their numbers grew. I attempted to lose them by joining a larger crowd of people that stood watching a quartet of musicians playing traditional Chinese string instruments. This was a miscalculation, for in a moment the musical quartet had lost its audience, which had deserted them to the last man for the superior attraction of a foreigner. Now I was trailing a band of the curious that would have been the envy of the pied piper. I had forgotten the lesson of Wuchow, that the world's largest undifferentiated racial mass, one billion Chinese, live in the Middle Kingdom, and that especially here in the interior I was curiosity enough to draw hundreds along in my wake.

I no longer felt that this milling mass, which by now numbered virtually all of the park's visitors, was following me. Rather it was driving me toward the main gate, back in the direction of the van. But everything changed when I turned about to get a picture to remember my pursuit by. As I aimed my camera at the crowd, it scattered like a herd of skittish deer. People continued to break for the wings each time I pointed my camera in a new direction. The mob's reaction was so unexpected, and so timid, that I almost burst out laughing. It was as if a giant, whom one fears on account of his size, had turned out to be crippled by shyness.

It was late afternoon and I had decided not to stop again. Rather, I would press on to Kweiyang before nightfall and then leave the following morning for Szechwan. At least that was my plan. It was not to be.

At a crossroads called Horse Flats, we were flagged over by a cadre wielding the now-familiar red flag.

"Is there a problem?" I asked.

"Very possibly," he replied, which is as close as a Chinese official will come to telling you that disaster threatens.

He told us to follow him and began walking up the street. We crept along behind him in the van like a water buffalo dogging the heels of his keeper. After a couple of minutes we came to a single-story brick building. The hand-lettered sign hanging horizontally alongside the doorpost after the Chinese fashion read: Kweichow Provincial Motor

Vehicle Inspection Bureau, Horse Flats Station. "Come inside and relax for a while." the cadre said to Ming. The invitation came out a little too casually and Ming gave me a small skewed smile before disappearing into the station. It was a look that had none of his usual jauntiness. I was left outside to wonder what was about to happen.

For a long time nothing did. The afternoon shadows lengthened into an orange dusk. The crowd of men that had inevitably gathered as soon as the van stopped stood stock-still, silently regarding me with the patient scrutiny of zoologists performing a dissection. Phlegmatic but intense, they were pressed up so close to the van on all sides that, had I wanted to get out and stretch my legs, it would have been impossible to open the door. I was trapped in the van as surely as if I had been locked in. It was not the first time that, like some strange new moon, I had drawn tides of blank, staring faces, but Ming's forced absence had me on edge. I wanted to take my camera out and see if they would scatter like my pursuers in the park, but I thought better of the idea. Instead I decided to sit motionless, thinking that the spectators would lose interest and drift away if the animal in the cage did not do tricks.

So I sat in the van, still and staring straight ahead despite my feeling of claustrophobia. One fly, then another, drawn by the crowd, came droning in through the window. At first I tried to ignore them. Then when their growing numbers made that tact impossible I tried to brush them away, but with as much economy of motion as possible, still thinking to bore the crowd into dispersal. Finally, to shut out the staring, collective presence that surrounded me and to make the time pass, I took out my notebook. But my notes were little more than a series of interrogatives:

> What did Ming do wrong? Is he being interrogated? Is he suspected of having committed a crime? If so, what? How long will they keep Ming? What is going to happen? I want to get back on the road.

Ming's familiar voice broke into my thoughts. He had pushed his way to the passenger window of the van without my knowing it, so completely had my worries overwhelmed my awareness of the human sea that lapped on my doors. "I thought that they were going to get me for speeding," he told me, "but it's you they want to see." There had been a phone call from one of the towns we had passed, and the public security department would be coming to investigate. "It was probably that turtle's son at the horse market," Ming offered brightly.

All the officer inside would tell me, and this in a gruff and overbearing manner, was that his unit had been notified to stop my van. For the rest it was sharp questions and suspicious glances, eyes peering out from under the olive-drab army cap that he kept jammed down low over his forehead. Where had I come from? Where was I going to? Why was I traveling through the countryside? Who had sent me? He recorded all of my answers in minute detail. Three times during the course of this questioning, the phone rang. Each time the official held the mouthpiece half covered and spoke in the choppy local dialect that I couldn't quite follow. I guessed that he was relaying the information he had gathered on me to the other party, who in turn fed him further questions to put to me, for the interrogation resumed anew after the end of each call. After hanging up the third time, he asked if I had a travel permit. He seemed rather nonplussed by what I showed to him. This time he didn't wait for the phone to ring but called himself. Two sentences of what ensued came through loud and clear. "He has a travel permit," I heard him say. "It says that his destination is Szechwan and that he has permission to travel by motor vehicle." Then he listened for a long time before putting the phone down.

The official was transformed. He courteously offered me a cup of tea, contritely apologized for delaying my trip, and told me that there had been a misunderstanding, that there had been a report of a foreigner traveling without permission. As soon as the prefectural public security office contacts the provincial office in Kweiyang and reports that I have a valid travel permit, I can be on my way, he assured me.

The minutes ticked by. The phone lay silent. Finally I wondered out loud if, since it was getting late and we were en route to the provincial capital anyway, we couldn't be on our way. "I can go to the provincial public security department tonight in person if there is any need," I said.

This suggestion led to another phone call, the upshot of which was that I could proceed on to Kweiyang, but only under escort. A local public security cadre would accompany me. The official, being Chinese, endeavored to put the best possible face on this turn of events: He suggested that it was for my own safety. "It's already dark outside."

The words came out with the gravest courtesy. "We wouldn't want you to get lost."

We sat in the van for another fifteen minutes until a slight, tousle-haired young man in the white good-humor uniform of the Chinese police came running up to the van. He had had to run home and fetch a change of clothes, he explained apologetically. He was hardly a sight to strike terror into the heart of a wayward foreigner, and I smiled as I told him to climb aboard. Although I was still anxious over what awaited me in Kweiyang, I was glad to be on the road again.

We arrived at the Yunyen Hotel in Kweiyang at 10:00 P.M. I was given a room on the second floor, but Ming was put down in the base-ment with the hotel staff. My unimposing escort, on the other hand, was to stay right down the hall from me, in a room that I noted was between my own and the stairs.

CHAPTER SEVEN

"This Province Is Restricted"

H<small>E</small> had come upon me at breakfast, a plump, pleasant-faced man who introduced himself as Comrade Wang from the local office of the China Travel Service. Wang was a professional tourist manager. His job was to keep foreigners—"foreign guests"—in line, arranging their itineraries, accompanying them to specially selected model schools and factories, ensuring that they saw only what they were supposed to see and heard only what they were supposed to hear about China. It was a job that required loyalty, discipline, and a gift for innocuous patter. I guessed that Wang was very good at what he did. He had politely refused my offer to order a bowl of rice congee for him and, exuding comradeship, talked endlessly about friendship between the American and Chinese people until I finished. Then he delicately broached his business.

"There is a problem."

I waited.

"The province of Kweichow has, er, not yet been opened to foreigners." Wang spoke in a halting whisper, as if he were afraid that he would be overhead divulging a state secret.

"You mean to say that the entire province is closed to foreigners?"

It was not a rhetorical question. We were talking about an area the size of Arizona.

"Kweichow is not yet open to foreigners," he repeated, anxious to put the best face possible on the restriction.

Closed or not yet open, Kweichow was clearly not the place for me to be at the moment.

"What about this city?"

"Kweiyang is open, but you must not leave the hotel."

Wang relieved me of my travel permit and stood up. He was going to have it stamped by public security. He would be back in an hour. Again came the warning: "Don't leave the hotel."

I went back to my room, a dreary place with waist-high wainscoting of dark wood and somber drapes that hung in thick folds down to the floor. In my present state of mind I found it suffocating. This must be what house arrest feels like, I thought. Except that it wasn't my house I was confined to. It was a strange room in an empty hotel in a forbidden province a thousand miles in the interior of China. Better to pack up my gear and wait in the lobby. That way, I said to myself, I could avoid the extra day's room charges that Chinese clerks, exhorted by their government to earn foreign exchange, are sticklers about. But this was just a rationalization. I was really just trying to escape the claustrophobia of my immobilization.

The lobby was colonial in its size, a vast receptacle of polished mahogany with the hotel office at one end and an overstuffed sofa at the other. It was a caricature of a couch, blown up by the inflated imagination of provincial Chinese about the physical dimensions of foreign barbarians to the size of a beached whale. I sank into one corner and stared across the sea of dark wood at the office. Over the reception counter I could just see the bobbing heads of the four clerks as they sat at work at their desks. These had been cozily pushed together to form a large rectangle. The better to kibbitz, I concluded from the hushed whispers that formed a background noise as continuous as the drone of a nest of bumblebees.

It did not take long for me to grow familiar with, then bored with, my surroundings. The Cloud Cave Hotel, for such was it called, was a well-maintained mausoleum. No guests came or went, and I saw no other staff except the clerks. The main doors—more dark mahogany—

were kept closed, their small glass panes separated by slats of wood that resembled bars. The panes themselves offered nothing more to the eye than a few snatches of the parking lot, empty except for my van, and of the high wall, which ran around the perimeter of the hotel and denied me a view of the street and the diversion of passersby. There were only the mysteriously busy clerks, and their endless whispered conversations.

Two hours passed. Around 10:30 a foreigner came down the stairs into the lobby. He was the first guest I had seen, and I would have liked to talk with him, but a blue-suited China Travel Service official herded him quickly out of the hotel and into a waiting car.

Except for this brief passage, the lobby remained empty. Ming was asleep somewhere in the bowels of the hotel. He had told me after breakfast that Chungking was still a long way away and he was going to bank up a little more shut-eye. I sat embedded in the sofa and watched the clerks at their desks, speaking continuously in low tones. I couldn't imagine what kept them at their desks all day in the empty hotel, nor what they found to talk about. The one time I went up to the counter, their conversation ended in mid-sentence, their faces awry. No, they didn't have very many foreign guests, said the one I had pegged for the head clerk. No, there are no tourist attractions in Kweiyang. Yes, there is an Institute of Geology that is located here in the city, a part of the Academy of Sciences, but that is all. He was polite enough, but his flat, expressionless eyes told me that he had no taste for conversation with me. He suggested that I go back to my room. I went back to the sofa instead, sinking into its grasp like a paralyzed fish into a sea anemone.

I don't think that time can pass more slowly than in the vacant lobby of an empty hotel in the interior of China. For a while I read desultorily in my notebook. There was nothing to add to it after I had brought it up to date with this morning's conversation. For a quarter of an hour I examined the hardwood floor for scuff marks. But mostly I just waited, and worried increasingly about why the China Travel Service official was taking so long to return.

It was clear what the problem was. I had stumbled into a restricted area. Like Tibet with its rebellious Tibetans, Ch'inghai with its large prison population, and Fukien separated by narrow straits from non-Communist Taiwan, Kweichow province was closed to the outside world. Of course the Kwangtung public security had known that I was coming this way but hadn't mentioned any restrictions on travel. Maybe they hadn't known. Maybe they had known but couldn't reveal the fact to me because the designation of "restricted" was itself a secret. Either way, it was not my fault. Why should I be held here?

I had been seen entering the province. Perhaps I had been reported by the same Ministry of Transportation personnel who had inspected my van and my papers. There was a Catch-22 quality about first allowing you to enter a province, and then a hundred miles inland arresting your forward motion on the grounds that the province was restricted. To my Western mind, such action constituted gratuitous harassment. But how would Kweichow public security view it? That's what worried me. I might be arrested for violating travel regulations. Or had I already been arrested? Wasn't my current detention something on the order of house arrest, a more comfortable cell to enjoy my confinement in? I didn't think that they would kill me or sentence me to labor camp. After all, Mao was dead and the spy mania of his days had receded somewhat. Still, I could be held indefinitely. That's what they did to Chinese prisoners. They held them until they produced an acceptable confession, then they charged and sentenced them in rapid succesion. There was no right to a swift and fair trial in the People's Republic. The determination of guilt was made by the public security apparatus. The trial came later, and was nothing more than the ritual administration of punishment. In the meantime, I was immobilized, imprisoned inside a world that I had, just a few hours before, been eager to penetrate.

It was already past eleven o'clock. The China Travel Service guide had said that he would be back in an hour. He was two hours late.

I tried to put myself in the place of the Chinese officials reviewing my case. A foreigner had entered a restricted area without permission. What should be done? The obvious solution was to eject the intruder as soon as possible. But who knew how long it would take them to reach it? I would volunteer to take an escort along with me until we were out of the restricted area and into Szechwan. If that wasn't satisfactory, then I would offer to take the train to Szechwan. The van could catch up with me later. There, that was certainly a reasonable solution, acceptable to any fair-minded official. I would go present it. True, Wang had instructed me to remain in the hotel, but he had also said that he would return in an hour. At best the matter would be resolved; at worst I would have another strike against me. Anything would be better than staying in this crypt of a lobby.

Energized by my decision, I fought my way free of the couch and went to look for Ming. I found him in the basement, occupying a cubbyhole the size of a wardrobe closet. "This is where the help sleeps," he laughed, shrugging on his jacket. Our escort from Horse Flats had gone back that morning, Ming told me, but he was sure that the provincial public security headquarters was nearby. He would ask for directions upstairs.

I had seen little the night before and I looked about eagerly as we swung out of the parking lot. Even knowing that Kweiyang had always been the smallest and poorest of China's provincial capitals, I was still unprepared for the largely empty streets I saw, devoid of motor vehicles and with only a few cyclists. Most surprisingly, the sidewalks were not thronged with people. This may not seem remarkable to an American, since U.S. city streets are often deserted, but I had never before been in a Chinese city in broad daylight where this was so. Compared with Canton, with its bustling fleet of used Hong Kong taxis (purchased on the cheap to handle the hordes of foreign tourists), or even Liuchow, with its hordes of little green tank carts and cyclists, Kweiyang seemed a ghost town.

The public security headquarters bore a close resemblance to a military encampment. It was surrounded by a high concrete wall topped with barbed wire, and armed sentries stood at attention on both sides of the main entrance. Inside was a central parade ground, where a company of what I assumed were new recruits was being drilled in formation. Further in, row after row of dormitories were visible, where the police and their families lived. There would also be well-stocked stores, where the police and their dependents could buy foodstuffs and other goods that were hard to obtain on the outside. I was reminded of the special riot police used by the Polish authorities to put down Solidarity. The Polish Zomo, as they were called, were similarly isolated from the general population and given special privileges to ensure their loyalty. The difference was that in China it was not simply a matter of a special riot force that was so treated, but the entire public security system. The county and prefectural departments of public security that I had seen had the same fortress-like air, the same resident contingents of police-men and their families; only the scale was different. Like their fellow Communists in Poland, China's powers-that-be wanted to be able to count on the unquestioned loyalty of its public security forces in the event of civil strife.

We were challenged at the gate, and Ming explained that we were looking for the foreign affairs department. We were told to get out of the van, and Ming was ordered to wait beside it while I was led into a low, whitewashed building immediately to the left of the gate by two cadres, one who walked ahead and one who walked behind. A door was opened and I was herded through it.

I found myself in a room deeper than it was wide. At the near end were four armchairs of the same bloated variety as the sofa I had spent the morning in. At the far end of the room, standing beside two desks, was a small group of cadres who stared at me when I was brought in with the expressionless eyes of their kind. I recognized the China Travel Service official among them, wearing an unhappy expression that seemed out of character on his genial features. He was able to manage only a faint smile when I greeted him, and it was another official who stepped forward and waved me to my seat. This man was only of medium height for a Chinese, but his thinness—he was so slight as to be nearly cadaverous—combined with a long neck made him appear taller. He was, as I found out later, Chou Chien-min, ''Establish the People'' Chou, the head of the foreign affairs office and the man who was to be my interrogator. He wasted no time.

''Explain your situation.''

''I am traveling from Kweilin to Szechwan.''

''What are you doing in Kweichow?''

''I am just passing through.''

''What do you do in the States?''

''I study at a university and write.''

On and on it went. I had to list all of the stops we had made, the horse market, the Duchun People's Park. (As I was to find out later, they were asking the same questions of Ming at the same time.) The questions began to be repeated. By the third repetition, I had had enough.

''What have I done wrong?'' I interrupted my interrogator. ''I have a valid travel permit showing that I have permission to travel by motor vehicle. I am en route from Kweilin to Chungking, Szechwan, two cities that I have permission to visit. The most direct land route from one to the other goes through Kweichow. I am sorry that I entered a restricted area but I didn't have any way of knowing . . . ."

"You have committed three violations," Chou cut me off. "First, foreigners cannot rent cars and go on long trips. Second, foreigners are not permitted in Kweichow. Third, you have broken the travel regulations of the People's Republic of China and must be dealt with."

This last had an ominous ring to it. I chose to ignore it and present my alternative.

"Since the province is closed, the main point is to get me out of it. Why don't you send an escort to accompany me out of the province?"

"Out of the question. Even if Kwangtung gave you permission to travel by motor vehicle, we in Kweichow can't allow you to travel within the province that way, escort or no escort."

"What if I took the train to Szechwan? My driver could travel alone to Chungking, my next stop, and I could continue my journey from there."

Now the China Travel Service official spoke up. "There is a train for Chungking leaving at around 6:30 P.M. I could purchase a ticket . . . ." He seemed eager to resolve the impasse, to smooth over the episode, and to speed me on my way. A crafter of impressions, he was probably dismayed by the heavy-handed way the police were treating me. It went against his training.

Comrade Chou strode over to the small, barred window and stood looking blankly out. Finally he appeared to reach a decision. Flatly, tonelessly, he began to speak: "You may take the train to Chungking. Your driver may take your van to the same destination. It will be up to the authorities in Szechwan whether or not you may continue your journey by motor vehicle."

I gave the China Travel Service official the money for the ticket—he had the fares memorized—and went back to the guest hotel to collect my luggage and wait. Everything had worked out well, almost too well.

Ming's mood was a reflection of my own, and we laughed together the laugh that is the spontaneous release of tension about our separate but identical interrogations. We had been friends since he had begun driving for me, but the challenges of this trip had forged a deeper camaraderie. As we returned to the hotel and prepared for our separate journeys, Ming grew talkative. Before he had been reticent about his past. Now, facing a separation, he told me more about himself.

"I was ecstatic when, seventeen years old, I was selected for the People's Liberation Army. It was a great honor. Only one other youth from my village was selected. It was the only way to leave the village, to escape life as a peasant. That was in 1966.

"After I completed my training as a driver, I was sent to Wuhan on the Yangtze River. For a while everything was fine. Then the Cultural Revolution began. The city was in anarchy. Workers and cadres were battling in the streets. But Mao wouldn't let us intervene. We were forbidden to keep order. All we did was go in after the battles were over. The corpses would be loaded onto my truck and I would take them outside the city where they would be dumped in mass graves. The death and destruction seemed pointless to me. Maoism wasn't building up China, it was destroying it. In Wuhan, it took several years to repair the damage caused by the turmoil of the late sixties.

"We were kept in the army longer because of the troubles, but by 1974 I was due to be discharged. I was looking forward to returning to my village. My whole unit—four thousand soldiers—was discharged at the same time, but we were not allowed to go home. Even though we were no longer in the military, we were still under its control. We were ordered to remain in Wuhan, assigned to a steel factory that was under construction there.

"Don't think that life in the cities is always good. If I had been from a mountain village I might have been happy. But I was from the Delta and I was not. At that time in Wuhan, fresh water was rationed, food was often unavailable, and the electricity was turned off every other night. The officials said that the city was industrializing too fast. The real problem was that priority was being given to industry. The people came last. It takes 100,000 gallons of water to produce one ton of steel. The people got to drink only what was left over.

"I married a woman from my native village as soon as I was discharged. We used to have water only three times a day in our factory dormitory apartments. An hour for breakfast, an hour for lunch and an hour for dinner. Even on the nights when we had electricity, they used to turn it off at nine o'clock. We were limited to one catty of oil a month, an amount that would last, even when used sparingly, less than two weeks. Meat was limited to half a catty [about half a pound] a month per person, and it was mostly pork fat. We used it mostly for oil. We could eat meat only once a week.

"My superiors repeatedly turned down my requests to return to Kwangtung, so I finally took matters into my own hands. My wife and I left for the Delta on our own, without official permission.

"We became 'black residents,' people without any household registration in the area they live in. I couldn't get any grain, nor could I work for the collective. I had to find another way to make a living.

"I found an old punt and managed to repair it. Every day I would row out on the West River and fish. The fish I caught I traded on the black market for enough grain and oil to feed the three of us, for by now my wife had had a son. It was only several years later that I was able to have my household registration transferred back to my birthplace."

Ming paused, and offered up his secret smile before concluding: "The only thing a man can do in this country is stay out of trouble with the authorities . . . and smile to himself at the absurdity of it all."

The conversation turned to practical matters. We were to meet the following day at the No. 1 Reception Center in Chungking. I would probably arrive first but Ming, who would leave immediately, should be there before nightfall.

After Ming drove away, I continued to mull over the man and his history. I thought that I finally understood the better part of Ming's cynicism. His peasant fatalism had been tempered by a canny intelligence into a vision of the human condition as absurd. In the weird, contorted politics of the Cultural Revolution, things made sense only if you first accepted the fact that nothing was making sense. It was a leap made by many Chinese, who independently invented an existentialist world view, without the aid of philosophers, out of the amalgam of their own experiences.

Ming was cynical and, about the things that mattered, disheartened, but he was not openly rebellious. His cynicism, his unwillingness to believe in any ideals, these things had unmanned him. He would not sacrifice even a modest measure of self-interest for any political convictions, because in his view such convictions are all, like the socialism he has known, fraudulent. He would merely smile his secret smile and go on his way.

Westerners are sometimes given to think that the PRC and other Socialist countries have succeeded in transforming their citizens into so many unthinking cogs going mechanically about their state-assigned business. This is false. Brainwashing exists, but it is such a labor-intensive, costly undertaking that it can be used only on relatively small numbers of the most worrisome political prisoners. The propaganda broadcasts, occasional political meetings, and short-term efforts at thought reform experienced by the majority not only are insufficient to create dedicated Communists, but actually serve to alienate people from the ideology in question, just as a less-than-lethal dose of infectious disease will inoculate rather than kill. Unfortunately, such propaganda has a wider effect as well, building a resistance to any and all ideals and beliefs, making people resigned, cynical, and—by default—self-centered. This effect must be recognized, even welcomed, by the Chinese political elite. For if you cannot create dedicated Communists from your people, at least you can prevent your people from dedicating themselves to other ideals or isms, like democracy or anarchism. People without hopeful expectations about the nature of government are easier to govern than those who have them.

I gave myself over to the monastic confines of the hotel lobby to wait out the hours until my train to Szechwan left. I estimated that it would be five hours before the China Travel Service official came for me, but only two had gone by when I saw the official disembark from his chauffeured car in front of the hotel.

I was about to joke about his promptness, but his first sentence put an end to any levity.

"They want to see you at public security."

"Is there a problem?" I asked, knowing full well that there must be, but hoping otherwise.

"Probably," was all he would say.

I was received very properly in the Foreign Affairs Section by Comrade Chou. He greeted me with an astringent formality, instructed his assistant to pour me a cup of tea, and invited me to sit down, niceties that had been neglected on my impromptu first visit. I noticed that the collar of his Mao jacket was even buttoned closed, the equivalent of a

Westerner putting on a tie. It all put me on my guard. Chinese officials become pictures of politeness when they are about to become unpleasant.

He handed me a copy of a permanent resident card for foreigners, asking me if I had seen it before.

"We have had word from Canton. They have communicated to the Ministry of Public Security in Peking that you were not given permission to travel by motor vehicle. Also that you were informed that Kweichow province was not yet open to visits by foreigners."

"But that's not true," I sputtered. "You have the copy of my travel permit. You can see that I had permission to travel by van. And if it were true that Canton had told me that Kweichow was off-limits, does it make sense that I would jeopardize a long trip at the outset by traveling into a restricted area?"

Chou ignored my outburst. Decisions had been made by higher levels. His job was to see that they were carried out. Nothing I said was of any consequence. My protests were irrelevant.

Chou stood up, assuming a stiff, almost military bearing. As he read from the document he held in his hand, his voice was flat, dry, the voice of a court recorder reading the judge's sentence.

"The People's Republic of China has found that Mao Siti [my Chinese name] has violated the travel regulations for foreigners. Mao Siti is not permitted to continue his trip to Chungking, Chengtu, Nanking, Soochow, and Peking. Mao Siti is ordered to take the train from Kweiyang and return to Canton. He is not permitted to stop en route."

He finished reading and thrust out his hand at me in a gesture so aggressive that it took me a second to realize that he was merely handing me back my travel permit. On the back, in severe calligraphy, and stamped with the official seal of the Kweichow Department of Public Security, was the same message he had just intoned. The series of cities that had been denied me read like a casualty list. But Chou wasn't done yet.

"Now you must write a confession." He said flatly, as if there was no doubt that I, when commanded to by the Chinese state, would write anything I was ordered to, be it truth or fiction.

"I have no intention of confessing to anything. I have committed no crime."

I would like to report that Comrade Chou was so taken aback by my intransigence that he gave way. But that is not what happened.

Rather, in the same flat tone of voice he repeated: "You must write a confession. This is what Peking has ordered."

"And what if I don't?"

"If you don't," he droned on, "you will not leave Kweichow."

I was to be held hostage to my confession. It was a threat that gave me pause, for it brought home the precariousness of my present position a thousand miles in the interior of China. I could be held on this remote plateau for however long it pleased the totalitarian state that governed it. No writ of habeas corpus would gain my release, for no such law existed in China, where constitutional rights and legal advocates to argue for the defense of those accused had been dispensed with in favor of summary state justice. No newspapers would write of my confinement, and no public opinion would force my release. As an American, I might be allowed to contact the U.S. embassy fifteen hundred miles away in Peking at some point, and the State Department might exert pressure for my release. But who knew how long that would take? I had had enough of the Cloud Cave Hotel, and I wondered if even less comfortable quarters might be in store. I just wanted to leave this city, which seemed to me more and more like a giant steel trap, ready to spring shut. It didn't take me long to come to a decision. The moment seemed ripe for a little indirection.

"Give me a pen and piece of paper." Comrade Chou permitted himself a slight smile as he nodded to his assistant to get the materials I requested. There had been no doubt in his mind, I knew, that I could be made to comply. The Chinese who landed in the hands of public security invariably did.

"It will be difficult for me to write it in Chinese." This was not true. I write Chinese easily. But it was necessary for him to think that I couldn't for my plan to succeed.

"You may write it in English," he replied. I had been sure that he would. Nearly to a man the Chinese are convinced, with some reason, that no foreign barbarian can ever master the complexities of their own hieroglyphic script, with its thousands upon thousands of different characters.

"What would you like me to write?"

This request, which he saw as abject surrender, caused Comrade

Chou's face to twitch briefly in a pale imitation of a smile. He began reciting my crimes: "I, Steven Mosher, have willfully violated the People's Republic of China's Travel Regulations for Foreigners, specifically articles . . . ."

For my part, I wrote: "I, Steven Mosher, deeply regret that the Chinese Ministry of Public Security is convinced that I willfully violated Travel Regulations for Foreigners, specifically articles . . . ."

Comrade Chou said: "Without obtaining permission, I undertook a journey . . . ."

And I wrote: "After obtaining permission from the Canton Municipal Public Security, I undertook a journey . . . ."

And so it went. Whatever Comrade Chou may have thought, I was writing not a confession, but a true account of my journey, and a defense against the false charges that had been leveled at me. I took the precaution of writing in as cribbed a hand as possible—being left-handed, it was just a matter of letting instincts rule—and by sprinkling my sentences with Latinisms, legalisms, and circumlocutions, made my prose as dense and unreadable as possible. It was a task that my academic training at Stanford University had well suited me for.

When I finished, a translator was brought in. As Comrade Chou sanctimoniously instructed me on the necessity for self-reform, this man set to work. His face was soon a mask of fierce concentration, as he went back and forth between my statement and the English-Chinese dictionary he had brought with him. I almost felt sorry for him. No English primer could have prepared him for the academic sludge that he was now wading through. He was still hunched over the desk half an hour later as I left with Wang for the train station. By the time Kweiyang public security understood the actual content of my "confession" —if indeed they ever would—I would be well on my way back to Canton.

The China Travel Service official was quite subdued as we drove to the train station. I was one foreign guest who would take away not carefully crafted impressions but raw scars left by the psychological caning I had received. He decided to salvage what he could.

"You must not judge China by the standards of the West," he opened.

"Whatever yardstick you use, you are a wretchedly poor and totally unfree society."

"Yes," he glumly seconded, "but you have to remember that things are better for the Chinese people than they ever have been."

It was a surprise to hear this minion of the state agree that China was poor and unfree. "Look, the question is not one of progress, but of how much progress," I responded. "Things are better for people in all countries of the world than they ever have been because of the industrial and technological revolutions. Over the last thirty years, the majority of the nations in the world have done far better by their people than China. You live in the fifth poorest country in the world in terms of per capita income."

But I did not want to debate China's progress or lack of it with a member of the China Travel Service. Whatever Comrade Wang personally thought, or came to think, as a result of our discussion, he would cleave to the state line out of fear and duty. He was, after all, a professional apologist for the current regime. Besides, I had another question that I wanted answered. Before I left Kweichow, I wanted to know why this province was off-limits.

My companion had a ready reply: "Kweichow is closed because it has a lot of military bases."

This was probably part of the answer. The Miao tribes have a history of rebellion, and in dynastic times the province had bristled with forts. But I doubted if it was the whole answer. I hadn't seen any military bases from the road, although I kept this thought to myself so as not to raise any more unnecessary suspicions. "My theory is that it is closed because it is one of the poorest parts of China," I said instead. "During dynastic times, officials were commonly banished to Kweichow. Peking doesn't want foreigners to find out how badly off ordinary people here still are."

Wang looked pained but did not contradict me.

When the train came, he walked with me to the platform and tendered a friendly and gracious goodbye. Under the circumstances it was a remarkable performance, but nothing could make me forget that I was being banished from Kweichow.

My compartment was a cramped four-berther. I swung my overnight bag onto the upper left rack (my suitcase was going back on the van) to mark it as my own, and sat down at the tiny window table. I hoped no one else would be sharing the compartment. I did not want

Day Five
The homes of the peasants looked organic, of a piece with their stone-age landscape.

Comparatively well dressed and assertive, rural officials make a study in contrast with the quiet folk they govern.

Two Chwang women bound for the open-air market many miles away.

At the market, buying and selling is carefully monitored. Here the woodcutters sit in their assigned area waiting for customers.

This old man's fur cap and Confucian gown hark back to an earlier style of Chinese dress.

Day Six

A mountain market town and commune seat. The sign reads in part:
"Kweiyang—242 kilometers ahead."

This was Mao country. It was primarily on the strong backs and stoic
endurance of peasants living in mountain hovels like this one that the
Communists rode to power.

Peasant homes in impoverished Kweichow were only a small step above the mountain hovels we had just left in Kwangsi.

Some of the homes were built up against the hills, reminding me of the cliff dwellings of the Hopi Indians.

A horse market in Kweichow with a Communist official keeping watch (center). All commercial activity in China is under the close control of the state.

A gaunt pony takes its afternoon meal along the roadside, its rubber-tired cart nearby.

Three officials in a motorcycle with sidecar, a common sight in China.

Villagers in their horse-drawn carts are forbidden to use those urban streets along which officials live and work. The sign in the background reads: "Carts strictly forbidden."

The scourge of China's roadways: Antique-looking, two and one-half ton trucks, copies of those used in World War II by the Soviet Army, dominate China's narrow country roads, forcing other vehicles to the shoulder.

House construction in Kweichow: A stone foundation raises the structure off the boggy ground, where several layers of mud brick bring the walls to window level. From there, wood framing covered with matting supports the thatch roof.

company; I wanted to be alone to sort out my thoughts and impressions of the past week.

Someone tried the door, found it latched, and began pounding on it. I opened it to find a middle-aged man in a baggy, rumpled uniform, the conductor. He stuck his head into the compartment, satisfied himself, and turned to go. "Will anyone else be in this compartment?" I called out. He glanced at me over his shoulder but said nothing. Except for the China Travel Service official I had left on the platform, it seemed to me that the Chinese, usually so friendly and helpful, had suddenly all turned rude.

I latched the door again and tried to relax in my solitude. I got out my notebooks—I had filled five in all—and thumbed listlessly through them. My mind wouldn't concentrate. I realized that I was waiting—hoping—for the train to start. I was more anxious about leaving Kweichow than I had realized. There had been enough threats and changes in schedules that I was on edge even now, fearing that someone might come and order me to disembark, telling me that my confession hadn't been satisfactory, or that Peking had wired with new instructions to send me north to the capital. My mind spun free, exploring all of the things that could go wrong.

There was a bump, then another, and the train began to shudder forward. It slowly, too slowly, slid out of the station, and began to pick up speed. A row of grey tenement buildings slipped by, then a long factory shed. Then it was out of the city and pounding through the countryside. I experienced a rush of pure joy. My brief incarceration in Kweichow was over, and I had extricated myself by my wits.

Being alone in the first-class compartment contributed to my sense of freedom, as did the regular clackety-clack of the train over the rails. I was soon to find out that I was something of a prisoner here too, but in the meantime the sight of the countryside hurrying by, the sheer thrill of motion, of escape, was reward enough. I opened the window and reveled in the gusts of cool air that burst in upon me. Soot from the coal-burning locomotive soon took the fun out of this game. I stretched out full length on the bunk and contented myself with the swaying motion of the car and the clank of the rails.

I knew that my sense of escape was largely illusory. I was still deep in the interior of China. Still, there was comfort in the fact that I was headed for the Pacific coast. Whatever happened when I arrived in Canton, at least there was an American consulate in that city, and the distance from Canton to Hong Kong—the outside world—was only eighty miles.

The train was moving at full speed now, and I started humming to myself. As if I had willed it into being, from somewhere close a song started up, loud and tinny, coming from a speaker high on the wall. The music was not what I had had in mind. I could not make out the words clearly through the scratching, but the strains were those of a revolutionary opera. The speaker was not equipped with a volume-control knob. Not this for twenty hours, I groaned. After a search, I discovered a tiny knob under the window table. I could not turn off the screeching praises of the new order, but at its lowest volume they were scarcely distinguishable from the rattle and clatter of the train.

I spent that evening on the train working on my notes, adding details still crisp in my mind. I reran conversations and decided whether a peasant's voice had sounded like a frog croak or a rasp. I thought of hills clawed red with erosion, the sun flashing on rice fields of deep emerald, the cool shadows of adobe villages, the pattern of peasant lives. I reflected also on my detention and interrogation by Kweichow public security forces and the pressure that had been brought to bear upon me to "confess my crimes." I had, I realized, seen both more and less than I had intended.

For a moment in Kweichow I had been stripped of the protective cocoon of privileges that surrounds foreigners in Communist China, and had stood as helpless in the grip of the public security forces as any Chinese. There had been no laws to quote, no lawyers to call, and no constitutional rights to invoke. I had entered China's heart of darkness—the lawlessness at the very center of Communist rule—and seen the Chinese state as it appears to the Chinese people: an arrogant monolith of unbounded power that has reduced the individual to utter impotence and terrified obeisance. If I had been, in the end, able to slip the knot, it was because I was a foreigner, permitted to write in a foreign tongue.

My trip had been short-circuited. I would not see the mighty Sanmen Gorges through which the Yangtze flows on its way to Shanghai and the sea, nor the great swath of muddy water that is the Yellow River. I would have to be content with pictures of the garden homes of Nanking and with others' descriptions of the walled dwelling places of Peking. But that really didn't matter, I reflected. My destination had never been a place but an answer to the question: What has the Chinese Communist Party done for the peasantry? That answer I now had.

CHAPTER EIGHT

The Road Back

I was awakened by a pounding on the compartment door. Jackknifing into a sitting position (I had slept with my head away from the door), I reached down and unlatched it, sliding it open a few inches. It was the conductor, his off-white uniform even more rumpled than yesterday; it looked as if he had slept in it.

"It is time for your breakfast," he announced.

I fumbled for my watch. It was 7:30 A.M. but I had gone to bed late and slept poorly, kept semiconscious by the noise and motion of the train. "I don't want any breakfast, thank you. I want to sleep." I started to slide the door closed but he held it fast.

"If you don't eat breakfast now, the dining car will close until noon."

"Then I'll wait until noon to eat," I said, anxious to end the conversation before the strain of carrying it on woke me up completely. I slid the door home—this time he allowed me—and flipped the latch.

I had just dozed off when the pounding began again. "Go away," I shouted, but the pounding continued. I swung my legs out into a sitting position and cleared my throat. Thus prepared to give the conductor a forceful appraisal of his character, I threw open the compartment door. It wasn't the conductor. It was a waiter from the dining car.

"Your breakfast is ready," he said.

"I didn't order any breakfast," I growled. This didn't deter him in the least.

"If you don't eat now, you will not be able to eat until noon," he clucked disapprovingly.

It would be more accurate to say that if I don't eat now I won't be able to get any more sleep, I thought to myself. This coddle-the-foreign-guest attitude was a double-edged sword. The suspicion groggily surfaced that they took pleasure out of this forced feeding. "I'll be down in a few minutes," I told him.

Breakfast consisted of cold eggs lying in a pool of congealed fat, burned toast turned spongy by the humid South China air, and a glass of milk that left a pungent aftertaste, as if the cow had been hand-fed on ginger. Given a choice, I would have gladly traded the lot for a nice bland bowl of rice congee. I returned to my compartment slightly nauseous and fully awake.

I was at loose ends. The days in the van had been a relay run across the face of China, a hectic series of stop-and-go encounters and images that had filled up my senses and my notebooks. Here I was being borne forward across the countryside in a steel cage, unable to call a halt. This is how the Peking regime prefers to keep foreigners, I thought, encapsulated and in motion, so they can neither come to grips with the Chinese way of life nor communicate their own. Shuttled from one urban bastion to the next by rail or air, they are allowed into the countryside only for short, well-chaperoned tours of the dead tomb of an ancient emperor or the frozen theatrical of a model commune. The merit of my journey was that I had passed freely through the cities and the countryside.

Yet the passages had been difficult as well, creating jarring contrasts that spoke of inequality and unfairness: the farm hut sloping crazily on its hillside plot of sweet potatoes versus the drab, regimented, but for all that solid blocks of urban housing; the faded, patched garb of the rustic as against the basic proletarian respectability of urban dress; the beggar children slinking in the shadows of the urban planned economy, unwelcome visitors from the "other" China, where peasant parents worked with hungry bellies, enduring to the next harvest. I was discovering how tired I was, how much I had been wounded and worn by what I had seen.

The landscape unrolled past my window like a scroll. The speed of my passage blurred nearby fields and farmhouses, blotting out close scrutiny and allowing only hurried glimpses of rural life. The train was no place for a miniaturist like me. From my window I could take in only the primary elements of the countryside, the endless alternation of villages and fields, and it was this I reflected on now. It was not difficult to read the land. Bottom land meant that peasants ended the year with a few yuan in their pockets, more if a city or town were nearby. Hill and valley signified subsistence, and higher elevations hunger.

From whatever vantage point it is viewed, rural China is not a place for those interested in free-form expressions of nature. The face of the land is too clotted with humanity, too contorted by its heavy task of provision. The proliferation of the human zone gives the landscape a significance beyond geography. To whatever extent it is gaunt or flush, coarse or refined, these attributes are the curse or gift of peasant man.

For the most part, those on the land are cursed by it. While the cities are bastions of a kind of shabby proletarian sufficiency, the countryside—China major—is haunted by the specter of a widespread and endemic poverty not seen in the West since before the industrial revolution. Most peasants can stay at most a few months ahead of starvation. For the majority of Chinese, life is a desperate struggle to feed yourself from the plot of land on which you were born, culminating in an earthen grave.

This is not easy for non-Chinese to understand. We dwell in the cities and, knowing them too well, judge them too harshly. "Hell is a city much like London," Shelley once wrote. "A populous and smoky city . . . . /Small justice shown and still less pity." For the metropolitan, hopelessness and poverty are defined by the derangement of an inner-city slum.

In the countryside we lose our bearings. We are not equipped to judge rural poverty and we lower our expectations, partly out of ignorance, partly out of a willful romanticizing of the pastoral. Bare feet in the city cry of a poverty beyond bearing; going barefoot in the countryside whispers of communing with nature. A Mexican barrio with its feeble huts of flattened tins and cardboard provokes us to demand social justice; a village of even more primitive huts made of packed earth and piled stones hypnotizes us into a desire for an existence similarly bucolic.

Those who have been peasants themselves do not share our delusions. However downtrodden the residents of Third World slums seem to us, in their own eyes they are the upwardly mobile, having left some time-forgotten backwater for the pulsating fringes of a modern city. Homes built out of the plastic, metal, and cardboard scraps of industrial society may look dubious to us, but they are, by any realistic standard, a sight better than a mud hut. Slum dwellers are in fact better fed, clothed, educated, and entertained than they would have been had they remained in the remote backwaters of their birth. This much should be self-evident. Surveys suggest that the ratio of urban to rural incomes in underdeveloped countries usually equilibrates at around 2 to 1. A greater gap galvanizes the peasants to come in such numbers that it is rapidly reduced; a lesser division is insufficient to uproot them from their native places. That emigrants to Mexico City or Manila or Taipei expect a significant improvement in their well-being should be self-evident. After all, they were not forced to resettle in these cities, any more than our own ancestors were ordered to move from rural Ireland to New York City, or from rural Mississippi to urban Detroit. All of these various movements were alike spontaneous and democratic, millions of individuals voting with their feet for a better life.

I was distracted from my thoughts as grey buildings suddenly blanked out the reds and greens of the countryside. We had entered another citadel of the rich and privileged. From the map I judged that we had reached the Hunan city of Shinhwa. (The name meant, "Newness.") We did not stop, for the train was an express, bound for the city of Chuchow, and in a minute we reemerged into rice paddy. As always, the transition from country to city was a sharp one, and now this made sense to me.

China stands alone among underdeveloped nations in that no slums disfigure its cities. Foreigners invariably draw the wrong conclusions from this, imagining that it implies rural prosperity and able municipal administrations. In actuality it is a testament to something quite different: the awesome reach of a totalitarian order. China's slums number in the hundreds of thousands, but they are hidden away in the vast recesses of rural China, out of sight of tourist and town dweller. On the road I had come across these slums again and again. They are the un-numbered villages and hamlets of remote mountains and valleys.

Peasants in China remain trapped within the time warp of their valleys. Like European villagers in the Middle Ages, they live and die within a few miles of their birthplace, cut off from knowledge of the out-side world. Like serfs beholden to the lord of their manor, they are in thrall to the totalitarian state, whose officials run every commune. And like slaves in ancient Greece, they are an exploited underclass, their labor the bulwark of the national economy. Since the 1950s, when the state took over control of all important production and marketing func-tions, the countryside has been run as a hacienda economy, a vast mosaic of plantations that the peasants are forbidden to leave. In effect, Peking has instituted a "homelands" policy for its peasantry, only the enclaves—communes—are smaller, poorer, and more restrictive than those found in the Republic of South Africa.

Though Peking has tried to cover up the truth by loudly and repeat-edly proclaiming its concern for the peasantry, there are no modern societies which have so deliberately created an underclass, and few which so thoroughly oppress and exploit it.

Why? Why would the Chinese Communist Party, which had billed itself as the party of the peasantry, so immediately set about exploiting this same group after coming to power? In part the answer is economic. In the early fifties the PRC adopted the Soviet model of economic development, charging the costs of industrialization in large part to the agricultural sector. It was a plan that blatantly favored the cities to the detriment of the countryside. Before beginning my trip, I had read a biography of Liang Shu-ming, the famous Confucian traditionalist and rural reconstructionist, a man who for decades had worked to improve the peasant's lot. In a little-known but revealing episode that occurred at the 1953 session of the Chinese People's Government Council at which Mao Tse-tung and other Communist leaders were present, Liang implied that the actions of the Communist Party were tantamount to betrayal. Like past rebels, once the Party had "entered the cities" it had "forgotten the villages." Urban workers were now "in the ninth level of heaven'' while the peasants had been condemned to the ''ninth level of hell.'' Premier Chou En-lai, the chairman of the session, immediately rose and attacked Liang's views. Undeterred, the old Confucian rose to speak again, apparently intending to defend his position. He never got the chance. Mao flew into a rage, wrenched the microphone out of Liang's grasp, and began to furiously curse him in the crudest language before the astonished assembly. Liang's solitary objection served only to get him villified in the next political campaign, and the five-year plan went forward as scheduled.[1]

As for the late Chairman Mao's supposed sympathies for the peasant, these seem to have been more rhetoric than reality. His oft-repeated assertion that agriculture would be the ''foundation'' of China's development was taken by foreign observers to mean that the Party would manifest a special concern for its putative constituency, the peasantry. The actions of the Party that he headed gave a different interpretation to his words, namely that, like the Soviet Union, the PRC would extract from the peasants the funds necessary to fulfill its ambitious plans to develop industry. An ancient Egyptian pharaoh may as well have said, ''Slave labor is the foundation of the pyramids.''

Just as Stalin squeezed the Russian countryside for the capital to construct his steel mills, so has the Chinese state borne down heavily on the peasantry. Although, for appearances' sake, direct agricultural taxes have been kept to only 4 to 8 percent of rural income, other ways have been found to generate revenue. The government has set mandatory quotas for grain purchases, forcing the peasants to deliver a large portion of their grain and other crops to the state at below-market prices. Nearly everything that the peasants must purchase from the cities, from chemical fertilizer and cloth to hand tractors and radios, is higher-priced and of lower quality than equivalent goods sold in Hong Kong and Taiwan. For example, the price of the 28-horsepower ''East Is Red'' tractor I had seen wrecked on the second day of my journey is more than twice the world price (not to mention that its axles have a tendency to buckle under hard use). Chinese peasants are paid less for their grain and other products, and pay more for industrial products, than any other villagers in Asia. So efficient is this system of indirect taxation in

[1] Guy Alitto, *The Last Confucian: Liang Shu-ming and the Chinese Dilemma of Modernity* (Berkeley: University of California Press, 1979), p. 1-3, 324-327.

rich, lowland areas like the Delta that the state today collects more of the value of peasant production than tenant farmers fifty years ago paid to their supposedly "parasitical" landlords and "feudal" government authorities. Nicholas Lardy, an economist at Yale University, exhaustively analyzed the available data and concluded that "the state transferred significant resources out of the agricultural sector over a sustained period."[2]

This bounty is quietly poured into industry. Lardy also estimated that in 1978 total state investment in agriculture probably did not exceed 3.3 billion, or less than 5 percent of the total output.[3] But in that same year, Peking claimed that it had reinvested 36.8 percent of its gross national product. Even allowing for the natural tendency to exaggeration and/or inaccuracy inherent in PRC statistics, industry obviously received the lion's share of these funds.

If the Chinese government acknowledged the special burden it has imposed on the peasantry, and if the funds extracted were being put to good use, there would be much less in these exactions to object to. After all, transfers of capital from agriculture into industry are one way in which an underdeveloped country like China attempts to modernize quickly. But this kind of admission has not been forthcoming. Rather, the official line has been and continues to be—against all evidence to the contrary—that villagers are charged low prices for factory goods, are given high prices for their crops, and are out of pocket only the low direct agricultural tax. A proposal by Chinese economist Sun Yeh-fang to eliminate one of these hidden taxes by raising the prices paid to farmers, perhaps even to the level of market prices, met with a cool reception.[4] Under Sun's plan, revenue levels would have been maintained by increasing direct agricultural taxes. This was a move that China's leaders were unwilling to make, since publicly revealing the magnitude of the agricultural tax burden would be ruinous to the country's reputation as

[2] Nicholas Lardy, *Agriculture in China's Modern Economic Development* (Cambridge: Cambridge University Press, 1983), p. 127.

[3] Cited in Fox Butterfield, *China: Alive in the Bitter Sea* (New York: New York Times Book Company, 1982), p. 251.

[4] "We Must Boldly and Confidently Grasp Socialist Profit," *Ching-chi yen-chiu* [Economic Research], Vol. 9 (1978), pp. 2–14.

an egalitarian, socialist state where peasants get a fair break, and could possibly lead to rural unrest as well.

But even this duplicity could be in large part forgiven had the funds so accumulated been well and wisely invested in China's future. Unfortunately, this has not generally been the case. The pouring of resources into smokestack industries unsuited to China's backward economy, the senseless replication of factories in cities distant from both raw materials and major markets, and, above all, the proliferation of fat housing, food, and welfare subsidies for workers and officials, all bespeak wasted resources. The Chinese leadership seems to believe that both heavy industry and its dispersal throughout the interior are strategically necessary, and with over one million Soviet troops stationed on China's northern borders there is certainly cause for legitimate concern. But I can conceive of no convincing economic, strategic, or ideological justification for an income differential between city and countryside of 5 to 1, nor for inflating the standard of living of workers and officials by means of generous subsidies while, at the same time, hidden taxes are depressing the standards of living of the peasantry. These subsidies are detrimental to the modernization program, have no conceivable strategic value, and implicitly violate the Party's commitment to the peasantry.

Ultimately, it is only self-interest that could have moved the bureaucracy to support a program of urban subsidies that are both economically irrational and ideologically distasteful. Chinese mandarins are no exception to the rule that, however radical their ideology, the bureaucrats of a country are always bourgeois and middle-class at heart. Not that the high-level cadres who actually approve each salary and subsidy increase for the urban minority benefit significantly in any personal way from these decisions. They receive ample rewards for their services already. But their assistants and secretaries, cousins and grand-nieces, chauffeurs and cooks—all of the people with whom they have regular contact—do benefit, for they are all members of the urban minority. On the other hand, few bureaucrats have any contact with members of the peasantry. Fewer still have ties of kinship or friendship with them, for if such ties existed, they would have long since helped these rural unfortunates to obtain urban household registration.

Having been granted, these subsidies are even more unlikely to be rolled back. Ch'en Yun, the foremost economist of the Chinese Communist Party, is aware that large state consumption subsidies for urban residents make little economic sense. He is nevertheless opposed to raising food prices for fear that this would create "a chaotic situation"—in other words, urban unrest.[5]

If rich, lowland areas like the Delta were to be exploited, then poor, highland regions like western Kwangsi were to be controlled. No one knows better than the leaders of the Communist revolution that the forces that brewed within these backward villages could topple dynasties. They wanted to make sure that no other political group would be able to tap the vast reservoir of rural discontent that had been the moving force behind their own revolution. The goal was to end for all time the age of Chinese peasant rebellions.

Serfdom, like slavery, is a mechanism for controlling agricultural labor. In Russia it was instituted several centuries ago after large landholders began having trouble retaining their peasants, who could escape their overlords by the simple expedient of moving into the vast wildernesses that everywhere beckoned, and serfdom was only abolished in 1864. In the PRC, serfdom was instituted in 1958 after the peasants began moving to the cities in large numbers, adversely affecting agricultural production and playing havoc with China's planned economy. The population registration law announced that year made it illegal for people to change their place of residence without government permission. Peasants were told in no-nonsense terms to stay put. They were to remain in their villages, tilling the land, fulfilling their grain quotas. This action may have benefited the bureaucrats, by making Chinese society easier to manage, and it may have benefited the workers, by reducing competition for limited urban facilities, but it certainly did not benefit the peasant majority, who found their already limited world more tightly circumscribed than ever before.

For impoverished peasants to be, in effect, forced to provide food coupons and other subsidies to relatively well-off workers and officials is a reversal of elemental standards of social decency. It is—and this is not an analogy—a system of food stamps for the wealthy paid for by the

---

[5] Teng Li-ch'un, *Study How to Do Economic Work from Comrade Ch'en Yun* (Peking: Chinese Communist Party Central Party School Publishing House, 1981), p. 92.

poor. That it should be a socialist (Communist) country that is perpe-
trating this rip-off should, I think, surprise few outside of the hopeful
minority who believe such states exist solely to administer social justice.
That the state in question is the People's Republic of China, which has
long and self-righteously held up its own treatment of its peasantry as a
model for the Third World, will, unless I am mistaken, surprise and
dismay a much greater number. The realization that the old Confucian
scholar Liang Shu-ming had been right, that there had been a far-
reaching betrayal of the most basic interests of the peasantry, certainly
startled me.

It had grown humid as we descended from the Kweichow highlands,
the cool mountain air condensing into the oppressive tropical heat of
Hunan. I opened the window. The breeze felt refreshing, for we were
moving fast enough through the increasingly heavy atmosphere for it to
cool. A long blast of incinerated air reminded me that the train was
pulled by a steam locomotive, and I looked down to find my clothes
flecked with tiny cinders. Trying to brush them off left long streaks of
soot.

After the bleak heights of Kweichow, the rolling Hunan countryside
seemed incredibly opulent, almost overly so. The emerald green rice
paddies were so lush that they hinted at decay, the two-story wooden
farmhouses so large that their roofs and eaves were bowed and warped.
It was in one of these ramshackle dwellings, not a hundred miles south of
here, that Mao Tse-tung had been born in 1893, the son of a rich peasant. It was his experience in that farmhouse—a tortured relationship
with a dictatorial father—that bred in him the soul of a revolutionary.
Mao left home at the age of fourteen, and by the time he reached the age
of twenty-one he had decided that the countryside needed to be liber-
ated. My trip through China more than half a century after Mao's decision had led me to the same conclusion.

What Mao had sought for the peasantry was a release from the family ties and feudal relationships that had weighed so heavily upon
himself—the domination of landlord over tenant, of family over individual, of man over woman, of superstition over all. In place of the
local landlord he installed state communes, in which ranking male
cadres made decisions about matters formerly left to the family and the
individual, and in place of superstition he installed the mythology of

communism, preached by those same powerful priest-cadres. Mao had promised liberation to the peasantry but, in an Orwellian reversal, had delivered something very close to enslavement.

My reverie had brought me to the Chuchow station, where I would catch the Canton Express southward. I swung my valise off of the bunk and started down the passageway. The disheveled conductor stood at the door. As I approached he shifted his body slightly, blocking my way. "Please wait here. It'll be just a moment."

The train was stopped dead in the station, and I watched in growing dismay as the rush of disembarking passengers slowed to a trickle. Finally, after the platform was clear, a security guard appeared, nodded curtly to the conductor, and I was allowed off the train. The guard took up a position slightly behind and to the left of me, ignored my effort at a greeting, and matched me step for step to the station house. "Soon" was all he would say about my departure. I began to feel a very dangerous element indeed.

"You will wait in there for your train," he commanded, pointing with his chin toward the first-class waiting room. It was a small room, its two windows shut despite the Hunan heat, its several chairs the overstuffed kind that would be impossible to sit on for any length of time in this weather. When I saw that it was empty as well, a distaste akin to that of a prisoner facing solitary began to rise in me.

"I would rather sit outside."

"You will wait inside. That is where the foreigners always wait."

Especially those who are to be kept under surveillance, I thought to myself. I did an about-face and sat down on the nearest outside bench. No fewer than five other station guards and attendants, seeing their comrade in trouble, came over and ringed my refuge.

"It's hot out here in the sun. You should go inside, where it's cool."

"When the trains come, you'll be in the way here."

"The benches are for people waiting for the next train."

"It is not safe for you out here."

I tried to maintain a Buddha-like detachment in the thick of this bullying, but as the minutes went by, my composure gradually eroded. Finally I turned on my tormenters. "How is China ever going to modernize if you Chinese spend all of your time worrying about where people sit?" This retort, with its suggestion that they were not doing enough for the all-important Four Modernizations, worked like water on the Wicked Witch of the West. They melted away without another word, though I glumly noted out of the corner of my eye that the first guard had assumed a watchful stance a few yards away. This spy treatment had reawakened my fears. From all appearances, the matter of my trip was not yet closed. I wondered what surprises awaited me in Canton. Still, for the moment I had gained a little breathing room. I forced myself to take an interest in my surroundings.

It would not have taken a trained Marxist to notice that the station, which was largely empty, was riddled with class distinctions. There was the waiting lounge for officials—which had almost doubled as my cell— and the straight-backed benches for workers; there was the restroom inside the station for officials (also used by station personnel), and a concrete outhouse across the tracks for workers. A peasant would have felt out of place. Not that the differences were demarcated by signs. Communist ideology demands a pretense of equality, not to mention that ordinary Chinese have been made so acutely class-conscious that actual signs would be redundant.

This is a continuation of the class struggle by other means. It is not a struggle consummated on a battlefield by clashing armies, but the insidious and never-ending effort of an entrenched bureaucratic class to refine the traditional classes—peasants, workers, and officials—into hereditary castes, and to assume total control over them. The new mandarins are not evil—any more than a cancer is evil—merely utterly self-interested. I was sure that they could give rational reasons for each step taken down the road to serfdom. How persuasive the arguments must have been against the state assuming responsibility for feeding, clothing, sheltering and employing the multitudes of unlettered villagers. Better to have them remain in the villages, inert, isolated, and minimally self-sufficient. How convincing must the reasoning have been for doling out these same benefits to urban workers, the true proletariat, especially when it was understood that in their concentrated numbers the workers represented a potential threat to the urban-based state that peasants did not. Better to lull them with bread and circuses. As for the officials themselves, were they not servants of the state, deserving the best that it had to offer? And what manner of subversion might they engage in were they not satisfied with their lot? So did the rational quest for bureaucratic control hollow the egalitarian dream into a feudal nightmare.

A few people began to collect on the train platform, and I was made glad by the illusion of company. It made me feel less conspicuous, less alone. Still unsure of when my train was to arrive, I decided to put the question to one of those waiting, more as an excuse for a little human contact than anything else. I walked up to a man standing near the tracks. He had his back to me and did not see me approach. "Excuse me," I said, touching him on the shoulder. He erupted in sudden movement, spinning down and away from my hand into a kung-fu crouch. His face was a tight, suspicious mask. I froze for a second, then put my hands palm out in the universal gesture of contrition. "Sorry," I offered in an apologetic tone of voice, "just wondering if you knew when the train to Canton was due." The moment could not be salvaged. He straightened up, gave me a final wary glance, and without a word turned on his heel and stalked off.

Nothing was more unconsoling to me in all of China than this animal encounter. I could understand and excuse the unfriendly attitude of the security guard, or even of the rumpled conductor, because I saw that they were just carrying out orders, but I was flayed to the core by a fellow traveler's total denial to me of civilized courtesy. I gave up trying to communicate and returned to my bench, feeling uncomfortably marginal, as if my very membership in the species Homo sapiens had just been called into question. I still didn't know when my train was due but told myself ruefully that there was no point in worrying about it. They would make sure that I was aboard.

Shadows stretched the length of the station by the time I boarded the Canton Express. Another conductor in a rumpled uniform—the train had left Peking two days ago—showed me to my quarters. It was again a four-berth compartment, and I noted with mixed feelings that two of the bunks were already occupied. Would I have company or be snubbed for the day it would take to get to Canton?

As it turned out, I had both.

I had just put my valise on top of the bunk when a gaunt, bespectacled man entered the compartment. He was, I found out in quick succession, a historian who had spent his life in the study of the Tang dynasty, a former political prisoner who had spent ten years in a labor camp during the Cultural Revolution, and a recently rehabilitated fellow of the Chinese Academy of Social Sciences. The compartment became a confessional and I a priest as he told of the sins that had been visited upon him by the Red Guards in the name of Maoism. It was a hurried, furtive confession, and it ended abruptly when the compartment door was flung open.

My other roommate had arrived, a portly official-looking type who dismissed us both with a nod and climbed into the berth above mine, where he lay staring up at the ceiling. Even flat on his back his remarkable girth was evident, fatty deposits that spoke of endless rounds of Party banquets. An uncomfortable silence—at least so it seemed to me—settled over the compartment. After the train started, the historian disappeared into the passageway.

The door had no sooner closed than a genial voice boomed out from the berth above: "Where are you from?" My other roommate worked for the Propaganda Department of the Central Committee of the Chinese Communist Party. Not surprisingly, he was more guarded than the first, at one point asking me, in a voice more suspicious than conversational, "Your Chinese is very good. Do you work for the American government?" And while he also decried the Cultural Revolution, he threw in a great deal of radical rhetoric about building socialism and made a pitch for the Four Modernizations. Still he was a lively conversationalist, and I enjoyed talking to him. But when the historian returned, he likewise fell silent.

And so it went. Although my two companions were friendly enough when they were alone with me, neither of them would talk to me when the other was present. Nor did they talk to each other, at least not when I was in the compartment. Like other Chinese, they had learned the dangers of casual chatter during past political movements. I found the silence unnatural, and decided to take a walk. Perhaps they would talk in my absence, though I doubted it.

I didn't get very far. The next car down the train was a "hard" sleeper—narrow wooden bunks with boards instead of mattresses. These bunks stood in tiers four high that were bolted at right angles to the car's longest dimension, leaving only a narrow aisle down the starboard side. It looked like a bookmobile, only where the books would have been there were people, lying curled up on the low shelves or, knees hugging chest, squatting in the narrow aisle. Like their baggage, which was piled everywhere, they remained still, realizing the futility of any attempt at motion. I reversed direction.

To the front was a "hard" coach—the lowest class of train travel—with straight-backed, barely padded benches running along a central aisle. It was equally impassable, crammed with homemade suitcases, bamboo baskets, and bodies. In a car that was designed to hold sixty passengers there were nearly double that number, compacted three and four to a two-man seat, pinioned shoulder to shoulder in the aisle. I was uncomfortable just looking at them, and I wondered what destination could be worth such discomfort enroute. Many of them had already spent two days and nights wedged in place, and had eighteen hours to go before they obtained release, yet I heard no muttering or complaints. Everyone simply sat, quiet and perspiring.

I struck up a conversation with a group of three young men sitting in the doorway. They were technicians on their way home to Canton for a visit, traveling from the northern factories they had been assigned to after graduation from college. The other passengers, they told me, were either workers like themselves, returning home for their yearly vacation, or lower-ranking officials without the clout to travel by soft sleeper or the cash to travel by hard. No, there were no peasants. They were amused by the question. "Where would peasants get the money to take a train trip?" The hard coach was the lowest class of train travel, but it was not the bottom of the social scale. Or maybe it was that the peasants were simply off scale?

We hadn't talked long before the train attendant materialized and suggested politely but firmly that I go back to my compartment and "rest."

"I'm well rested, thank you."

"Well, you can't stay here," he said, irritation showing. "You're blocking the aisle."

I returned to the relative luxury of the sleeping compartment, where the Party propagandist was still stretched out comfortably on his back. He had talked a great deal about the Four Modernizations, how the program would modernize China and improve the lot of the Chinese people. I was not so sure. It seemed to me that the fate of the two Chinas—urban and rural—might be quite different. The Teng regime is betting its limited stake on urban-centered industry. With technology imported from abroad, the obsolete machine civilization of cities like Liuchow and Kweiyang can be gradually modernized, especially if access to Western markets is increased at the same time. With a generation of hard work, a hundred and fifty million Chinese concentrated in a few thousand cities and larger towns might attain the standard of living of the poorer parts of Eastern Europe.

But what of China proper, the eight hundred million peasants who still pass their lives in a timeless world of subsistence agriculture and handicraft commerce? To them, the Four Modernizations program has little to offer except a return to family farms and exhortations to self-reliance. This is, it must be admitted, a considerable improvement on the forced collectivism of Mao's time, and under the new policies the peasants of some areas have been able to help themselves. Those communities within walking distance of cities and towns will continue to prosper, their economies tied to the fortunes of the urbs in which they market their vegetables and handicrafts. Villages in rich lowland areas like the Pearl River Delta also have a margin of subsistence that if wisely invested will better their lot, though any improvements will come with painful slowness.

Away from the deltas and rich river valleys, it is another story. Shouting slogans about agricultural mechanization in villages like those I visited in Kwangsi is akin to advising a drowning man, from a position safe on the shore, to take swimming lessons. The peasants' poor, sloping fields produce only enough to keep them alive until the next season. There is no surplus to accumulate. Where could the money to purchase machinery possibly come from? Even if the state were to make an outright gift of farm machinery to such villages, the residents could not afford to operate it. Human labor is so cheap and plentiful in China that, as one discouraged village head told me, it would cost more to fuel and maintain the machine than it would to have the work done by hand. The fields I had seen would scarcely repay the investment of a water buffalo, much less of chemical fertilizer or a tractor. Ming was right. It was a joke to think that such places could modernize. Teng's goal of a per capita income of 800 yuan by the year 2000 would be laughable were it not so cruel.

After wasting a generation on fruitless political campaigns, China's leaders are desperate for development. The main stumbling block is that there are 600 million superfluous peasants living in poverty. Rather than concentrating its efforts on helping the rural poor, the current government seems interested only in paring back their numbers. Each couple in China is permitted to have only one child, a stricture that is enforced by means of forced abortions and sterilizations. The result of this stringent program of population reduction will be that after one generation the peasant population will be reduced by half, after two by three-quarters. In the meantime villages have become holding camps, places for hundreds of millions of peasants to live out their lives without being a burden on the state.

CHAPTER NINE

At the Canton
Public Security Office

I had been writing for hours in the small, stifling cell where they had put me, and had lost track of the number of times I had rewritten my confession. My writing hand cramped again and I put down my pen and massaged it for a few seconds, mindful that the guard would be on my case if I paused too long. There, it was done. I signed my name to the latest version and handed it over, hoping this time that it would be found satisfactory. My hand was more numb and cramped than ever, and I returned to rubbing it.

Suddenly Comrade Chou of the Kweichow public security office was standing in front of me, his face dark. He flung my latest confession on the floor. "This is totally unsatisfactory," he shouted. "We told you to write a confession, not a defense. You must admit that you were spying on your trip. Until you do, you will not leave." He continued shouting, but I could no longer hear his words over the pounding of my heartbeat. Even his image seemed to be fading.

I woke up in a sweat, momentarily disoriented in the grey, predawn light. The regular clackety-clack of the rails told me that I was still on the train. I had had a nightmare. My left hand—my writing hand—was stiff and numb. I had been lying on it.

The remainder of the morning I worked on my notes, or at least attempted to. The closer we got to Canton, the more difficult it became to concentrate. I was looking forward to returning to that comparatively bright, bustling city, a world removed from the grey, regimented pallor of Kweiyang. Of all China's cities, Canton was the one that I felt most at home in. Yet I was also apprehensive, wondering what the next stage of my punishment would be: expulsion or worse?

In Canton I was met as I stepped off the train by a public security officer holding a clipboard.

"Are you Mao Si-ti?"

"Yes."

"You are ordered to go immediately to the Canton Public Security Office."

For a tense second I thought that he intended to escort me there, but all he did was make a notation on his clipboard and turn away.

An hour later I stood in front of the same public security office from which my journey had begun. Only in coming here from the train station I had made a slight detour. Officials at the local American consulate now knew my whereabouts, and would raise questions with the Chinese if I were to disappear. Copies of my travel permit were on file, evidence that I had received official permission to go by van where I did. Now it was time to bring my trip full circle.

I entered and announced myself to the desk clerk. Shortly, the same public security cadre who had dealt with me nine days before appeared.

"Your travel permit," he snapped. I held it out. He practically snatched it out of my hands. He turned to go.

"Wait a minute," I started to ask.

"You may go," he said, interrupting me.

"Don't you want anything more?" I continued, still confused.

"No. No. You are free to go," he said, waving me off.

All they wanted was my travel permit. A feeling of relief washed over me, only to be quickly replaced by anger. They had been contacted by Kweiyang public security, and they had lied about the fact that they had given me permission to travel by van. All they wanted now was to regain possession of the one document by which I could prove them false.

The official was already halfway up the stairs when I called out.

"I have a request." I waited until he came back down the stairs and stood before me before continuing. "I would like to get a copy of my travel permit and also of the application form I filled out for same."

"That's unnecessary," he said.

"Then I want to talk to your section chief."

"He is very busy."

"Then I will wait until he is free," I said, sitting down at the table where I had earlier filled out my application form for a travel permit.

A long time went by. Twice the official appeared at the head of the stairs to see if I was still waiting. Twice he disappeared again before I could speak. Finally a portly official appeared at the head of the stairs in the company of two other officials, one of whom was the man I had spoken to earlier. This little entourage descended the stairs and seated itself across from me.

"I understand that you would like a copy of your travel permit and application form," the section chief, whose name was Liu, began in a most avuncular manner. He placed my travel permit on the table between us.

"Yes," I replied.

"I really don't think that is necessary," he said, sadly shaking his head as if it pained him greatly to deny my request.

"I think it is," I insisted. I had decided to be forthright about my reasons for wanting copies to see how he would respond. "You see, the reason given by the Kweichow public security office for canceling my trip was that I had entered a restricted area and according to them did not have permission to travel by van."

Section Chief Liu registered polite incredulity before saying: "Now that's not true. We gave you permission to travel by van. And according to our travel regulations, you have permission to transit a restricted area en route to your destination. You had to travel through Kweichow to get to Szechwan." His voice was calm and reasonable, his head thrust forward slightly to lessen the distance between us, and his eyes rested steadily upon me. He was the very picture of official probity. His mellifluous voice dropped half an octave to indicate sincerity as he concluded: "The reason your trip was canceled was because you did not immediately register with local public security upon arrival in Kweiyang City. By failing to do so, you violated our population registration regulations. This unfortunate oversight on your part led to your trip being canceled."

He seemed so convinced of what he was saying, so intent on trying to clear up my misunderstanding, that he almost had me believing that I had brought on the whole episode myself by failing to register. Then I remembered the obvious.

"But I arrived in Kweiyang late at night under escort by public security. My travel permit was taken to the public security office first thing the following morning for registration."

Section Chief Liu smiled indulgently. "It is the foreign guest's responsibility to register with public security immediately upon arrival, not public security's responsibility to register the foreign guest." He repeated, in the same friendly, almost patronizing way, that if I had only registered upon arrival in Kweiyang, all subsequent unpleasantness could have been avoided. There seemed to be no rebuttal to this argument. Then my eyes fell upon the travel permit that lay between us.

"Comrade Liu, the travel permit itself states that travelers have twelve hours in which to register with the authorities." I pointed out where this was written on the travel permit.

I have to hand it to Section Chief Liu. He didn't even blink when confronted with the travel permit. He even had the gall to try once again to convince me that everything had happened through my own negligence, as if to wear me down by repetition, as water wears down a rock.

But now I was on to him. I knew that he was lying to cover up his own responsibility for having given me permission to travel by van in the first place. And then I did something that I had wanted to do every time I sat across a green, felt-covered table from some suave, practiced official who was exaggerating production figures, or lying about birth-control policy, or the like. I said, keeping my voice carefully level, allowing no trace of anger or irritation to show: "You are talking nonsense."

Comrade Liu's associates went open-mouthed with astonishment. Liu had better control; he merely blanched slightly.

"You are talking nonsense," I repeated. "You know perfectly well that you gave me permission to travel by van and that this upset Peking and led to the cancellation of my trip. But you don't have the integrity to admit it."

The section chief's underlings had recovered from their shock by now and were bouncing up and down in their seats like little jack-in-the-boxes, all the while screaming: "You can't talk to our boss that way. You can't talk to our boss that way." Liu said not a word but, under their covering fire, found his way to his feet and beat a hasty retreat, closely followed by his still-agitated assistants, who all but stuck out their tongues at me.

I would have left for Hong Kong that same day if I hadn't been worried about Ming. It wasn't the long trip back from Kweichow that concerned me—he was an experienced driver, used to traveling solo—but the thought of what he might suffer at the hands of the Kwangtung public security apparatus after he arrived because of his association with me. I checked into the Eastern Hotel in Canton and began my vigil.

A week passed before Ming showed up, looking drawn and haggard. As I had feared, he had been taken into custody by public security following his return to Kwangtung. For three days he had been interrogated about my trip. What was it that I had been looking for, he was asked repeatedly. He had replied that I was just traveling for relaxation after my research, interested in nothing more than a little sightseeing. Finally, he said, they had lost patience with him and tried to pressure him into signing a statement they had drawn up that accused me of spying. So far Ming had been speaking in a rather listless manner, but now he straightened up and flashed that trademark grin of his: "I refused. I told them that it wasn't true."

After Ming had left, I thought about these suspicions that I had been engaged in intelligence work. I had to admit that, from the standpoint of xenophobic, secretive Party leaders and public security personnel, I was a spy, prying into areas that were officially proscribed, revealing things about the dark underside of Chinese society that the Party would rather not have come to light: how the bond between city and countryside has been cut, and walls of regulations erected in its place; how the peasants of the lowlands are exploited to provide foodstuffs to pampered urban residents, while expected to meet their own needs without government assistance; how absolute deprivation and malnutrition are widespread in the highlands, conditions that have been aggravated by government policies that inhibit internal trade and migration.[1]

The China I had seen didn't fit any of the standard political labels. It was socialist, petty capitalist, or feudalistic depending on where in the country you happened to look. Socialist was the designation preferred by

[1] Nicholas Lardy, piecing together the few available statistics on rural China, reached similar conclusions. See *Agriculture in China's Modern Economic Development* (Cambridge: Cambridge University Press, 1983), p. 186.

the Chinese Communist Party, but only the urban population, perhaps 15 percent of the whole, actually live under a socialist system. Outside of the cities, China wasn't a socialist country. Teng's rural reforms have returned a modicum of economic autonomy to peasants, who now can peddle their goods in the free market, start small businesses in their villages, and hold stock in collective-owned enterprises. Here again, it would be a gross error to take these capitalistic practices as indicative of China as a whole (and even less of her future), for they are found primarily near the cities and in the rich lowlands, and even there are closely regulated by the state. The majority of the peasants are not in a position to benefit much from either urban socialism or suburban petty capitalism. In the hills of Kwangsi and Kweichow I had found the villagers living under a system that most closely resembles a kind of state feudalism.* The only firm conclusion that can be drawn concerning this hodgepodge of different economic systems is that none of them has done much for village China.

To be fair, there is little that any economic system can do for a peasant on his half-acre as long as he remains a peasant. It is only upward mobility, the movement from peasant to farmer to factory worker to tradesman, that can truly change his life for the better. Such opportunities have come with painful slowness in the PRC. In 1949 Chairman Mao announced the creation of a "New China," but most of his countrymen continue to spend their lives in stoop labor. After three decades of land reform and agricultural collectivization, the countryside remains as poor and densely populated as ever. Instead of encouraging peasants to better themselves, household registration laws, production quotas, and ration cards seem to have been devised with the opposite purpose: to keep them on the land. "Born a peasant, die a peasant," is the essence of the PRC's class status laws.

The day after I saw Ming for the last time, I boarded the Canton-Kowloon Express for Hong Kong. Ming's safe return had brought my

---

*On November 17, 1984, the English-language *China Daily* published a startling and unprecedented admission of backwardness and poverty in Kweichow province. "Many people in Kweichow have barely enough food and clothing. . . . A third of the rural population is illiterate. There are far from enough roads . . . and they are the poorest in the country. Many regions cannot receive radio and television broadcasts and have no access to mail or newspapers." All in all, the report concluded, conditions in Kweichow thirty-five years after the liberation are "shocking."

quest to its end, and there was nothing more to keep me in Canton. Although I had not been bothered by public security again, and my visa still had a week to run, after the events of the past few days I did not feel entirely comfortable remaining in China.

The train rolled through the countryside under the glare of a brilliant midsummer's morning. From the comfort of my air-conditioned coach I could see the flooded rice paddies of the Pearl River Delta. The transplanting of the second rice crop was underway, and rows of peasants advanced across the fields, backs bent nearly level to the ground, thrusting their seedlings into the mud. Rooted hand and foot in the earth that fed them, they had the blind look of parasites. You felt that if the world were suddenly turned upside down, they would still be clinging to it, still crabbing along in the grasping mud within their appointed squares. As long as there are peasants, with their huts, their fields, their families, and their graves, there will not be an end of the Old China.

Epilogue

I left China thinking that the episode of my journey was closed. My travel permit had been canceled, but I had not been expelled from the country. I had been forced to write a "confession," but imprisonment had not followed. As for myself, another rural research project awaited me in the Republic of China on Taiwan. After I arrived in that country, I put the notebooks I had kept during my trip aside and began writing my Ph.D. dissertation for Stanford University. But, unbeknownst to me, forces had been set in motion by my journey that would yet play themselves out.

The first straw in the wind came when I heard, six months later, that high-ranking Communist Chinese officials had whispered to a visiting American academic delegation that while in China I had gathered large amounts of secret documents and sensitive information. It came out that the Ministry of Public Security in Peking had, in its own ponderous fashion, declared me to be an "international spy." As the months went by, this campaign of slander gathered force as each visiting U.S. academic delegation was subjected to a recitation of my "crimes against the people."

In 1982 the allegations took even more concrete form, as the Chinese government sent a document to my university, Stanford. Among other things, they claimed that I had overstepped the bounds of my research program in reporting on China's program of forced abortions, and claimed that my trip into the interior had been taken without official permission. Deal with Steven Mosher "severely," they demanded; otherwise, it was hinted, the scholarly exchange program would be cut back. To my surprise and consternation, these false charges were taken seriously by many at Stanford University. "It would be salutary," the *New York Times* had editorialized at the time, "if academic ranks had closed against a tyranny that aims to hide the truth and impose its standards on a free university."[1] Instead Stanford chose to expel me from the Ph.D. program.

In reporting on conditions in China, I had made powerful enemies. First among these were obviously China's rulers, who were concerned about the loss of face and political legitimacy that will ensue when it becomes generally known that the revolution has passed the peasantry by in its drive for industrialization. Closer to home, censure came from some academic quarters, particularly Stanford University. It is difficult to know whether some faculty members at Stanford were upset more because they were uncomfortable with criticism of self-proclaimed "socialist" states, or because they were worried that China would carry out its threat to cut back on research opportunities for American scholars in that country beginning with their own institution. The strain of cultural relativism that runs through American social science was undoubtedly also a factor. Many academics hold strongly to the isolationist view that whatever a foreign political elite decides to do in the name of its people is above criticism, even if, as in the case of China, the social agenda in question contributes to the pauperization and unhappiness of large numbers of the population.

There is always a cost in making public an unpopular truth. In my case, the price exacted—my effective disbarment from the scholarly profession of my choice—has been painfully dear. I went to China largely unaware of the risks of trying to do open research in a closed society, and of the professional dangers of daring to criticize the powerful. Had I been fully aware of how serious the consequences would be, the decision

[1] "Mosher vs. Stanford," *New York Times* editorial page, March 19, 1983.

to speak out would have been an agonizing one. But I trust that I would not have remained silent.

The most important role of social science inquiry is to demythologize the world, to allow us to see a society for what it is, rather than what various groups of self-interested bureaucrats and politicians of whatever political stripe say it is. If China's rulers prattle endlessly about their concern for the peasantry but covertly adopt policies that disadvantage this group—the vast majority of China's population—then the scholar who uncovers this fact has no choice but to report it, whatever the personal consequences. Social science has a right, no less than a duty, to take a critical and objective stance toward all societies, however powerful, monolithic, or threatening.